So begins the MBA Oath, conceived in early 2009 by Max Anderson, Peter Escher, and a team of Harvard Business School students. They saw that in the wake of the financial crisis, the Madoff scandal, and other headlines, ed. People were angry beca ny of whom were MBAs, see nything beyond their own private interests. Many began to question the worth of business schools and the MBA degree.

The oath quickly spread beyond Harvard, becoming a worldwide movement for a new generation of leaders who care about society as well as the bottom line. Thousands of graduating MBAs have now pledged to conduct themselves with honesty and integrity, just as medical students swear the Hippocratic oath before they can practice.

This book is the manifesto for the movement. It provides not only a strong case for why the MBA Oath is necessary but also examples of how it can be applied in the real world. It will help guide businesspeople through some of the toughest decisions they'll make in their careers.

The

MBA
OATH

The
MBA
OATH

SETTING A HIGHER STANDARD

FOR BUSINESS LEADERS

Max Anderson and Peter Escher

PORTFOLIO

PORTFOLIO

Published by the Penguin Group

Penguin Group (USA) Inc., 375 Hudson Street, New York, New York 10014, U.S.A.

Penguin Group (Canada), 90 Eglinton Avenue East, Suite 700, Toronto, Ontario,
Canada M4P 2Y3 (a division of Pearson Penguin Canada Inc.)

Penguin Books Ltd, 80 Strand, London WC2R 0RL, England

Penguin Ireland, 25 St. Stephen's Green, Dublin 2, Ireland
(a division of Penguin Books Ltd)

Penguin Books Australia Ltd, 250 Camberwell Road, Camberwell, Victoria 3124,
Australia (a division of Pearson Australia Group Pty Ltd)

Penguin Books India Pvt Ltd, 11 Community Centre, Panchsheel Park,
New Delhi – 110 017, India

Penguin Group (NZ), 67 Apollo Drive, Rosedale,
North Shore 0632, New Zealand (a division of Pearson New Zealand Ltd)

Penguin Books (South Africa) (Pty) Ltd, 24 Sturdee Avenue, Rosebank,
Johannesburg 2196, South Africa

Penguin Books Ltd, Registered Offices:
80 Strand, London WC2R 0RL, England

First published in 2010 by Portfolio,
a member of Penguin Group (USA) Inc.

1 3 5 7 9 10 8 6 4 2

LIBRARY OF CONGRESS CATALOGING IN PUBLICATION DATA

Anderson, Max.

The MBA oath : setting a higher standard for business leaders / Max Anderson
and Peter Escher.

p.   cm.

Includes bibliographical references and index.

ISBN 978-1-59184-335-1

1. Business ethics.   I. Escher, Peter.   II. Title.

HF5387.A63 2010

174'.4—dc22

2010001960

Printed in the United States of America
Set in ITC New Baskerville
Designed by Chris Welsh

Dedicated to the MBAs of the class of 2009

Contents

I

THE PROFESSION

II

THE PRINCIPLES

Acknowledgments

Although our two names are on the cover of *The MBA Oath*, both this book and the oath itself are the products of the tireless and selfless work of a number of individuals whom we would like to thank. We are inspired by the many MBAs from around the world who signed the oath and believe in its standard for business.

We are grateful to Nitin Nohria and Rakesh Khurana for their vision, inspiration, and leadership in the project of creating a professional oath for managers. Years before we began working on the MBA Oath, Nitin and Rakesh were already writing about an oath for business and making management a profession. From the beginning they encouraged us to build on their work but never once did they demand credit for their intellectual paternity of the MBA Oath; they were willing to put the greater good ahead of their own narrow ambition. Thank you. For everything.

We want to thank our classmates and friends who led the creation of the MBA Oath movement. This project would not have happened without them and they deserve to be recognized. Teal Carlock was the first person to volunteer his time to creating the oath. He and Max formed a partnership and they launched the oath together. Teal, thank you for your leadership, your loyalty, and your friendship.

In addition to Teal, four other classmates have worked with us as the executive team for the MBA Oath. Jon Swan, Dan Moon, Kate Barton, and Humberto Moreira. We have spent countless hours working together. Thanks for your leadership. We feel lucky to have had the excuse to stay in frequent contact postgraduation. We're looking forward to more.

A larger group of our friends have also continued working on the oath after graduation and we are thankful for their heavy lifting in the summer and fall to both lay out the strategy for the MBA Oath and to help edit this book—Sandeep Acharya, Diane Averyt, Rye Barcott, Mohit Bathija, Paul Buser, Alla Jezmir, Andrew Klaber, Umaimah Mendhro, Dalia Rahman, Thomas Rajan, Maura Sullivan, and Eric Tung. In all, thirty-four classmates worked together to make this a reality. For helping us draft the initial language and for helping launch the MBA Oath at graduation, we also want to thank Patrick Anquetil, Elana Berkowitz, Brian Elliot, Eric Erb, Adam Heltzer, Drew Jackson, Kevin Meyers, Andy Morse, Sunil Nagaraj, James Reinhart, Ben Reno-Weber, Garret Smith, Scott Spencer, Mark Tapper, Jimmy Tran, and Michael Wick.

Our gratitude also goes out to:

The dozens of members of the MBA class of 2010 who have already taken up the torch to continue building the MBA Oath, especially Larry Estrada, Adam Ludwin, Albert Norweb, and Whitney Petersmeyer.

Bill George for generously supporting the MBA Oath both financially and with his advice. He is a good friend and has been an invaluable mentor.

The faculty and administration of Harvard Business School

for their support and encouragement and for giving us a deeper appreciation for business ethics.

We are also grateful to have been a part of the creation of The Oath Project, a new effort to build on the success of the MBA Oath and other efforts to reach students and business leaders worldwide. Our partners there include Rich Leimsider and Judy Samuelson at the Aspen Institute, Thunderbird dean Angel Cabrera, and HBS's Rob Kaplan.

Ike Williams, our agent, and the team at Kneerim & Williams for introducing us to Portfolio and keeping good spirits. Our editor, Adrienne Schultz, for shepherding us through this process. Our publisher, Adrian Zackheim, for seeing the value in this project. Everyone at Portfolio who has worked double time to get this book out in a short time frame.

Personal Acknowledgments

Writing a book, I have found, requires all of you. In fact, it requires a lot from your friends and family as well. I count myself blessed to have had an all-star team on my side. I first met Peter on a first-year business school trip to Seattle. We have been friends ever since. He is wonderfully straightforward, deeply thoughtful, and he is willing to stand in the gap. I'm grateful for working with him. He made it possible.

Jess, you read every word. Multiple times. And when I felt I could no longer walk, you carried me. It is a privilege to be married to your best friend. I love you.

Carolina, you make me feel like the luckiest daddy in the world. My favorite book is whatever I'm reading to you.

Pop, you are the best writer I know. You swam as far as was needed. Mom, you made me believe I could do this.

Anna, you are a gifted writer. Thank you for listening, for reading, and for your friendship. Auntie Linda, you read and responded to the book in its early form and boosted me along the way. Mike and Jocelyn, you were patient and you babysat while Jess and I edited. Thank you. All my extended family, your support and prayers are invaluable. Finally, my grandfathers, Leonard and Elwood, who taught me the meaning of personal character and professional integrity in the way they ran their businesses.

I would also like to thank: Section J for making business school so rewarding; David Gergen and the staff at the Center for Public Leadership for helping me develop my thoughts on leadership; the cheese plate club; the Hiwassee group; and the many who have reached out with encouragement along the way. Clarence was right. No man is a failure who has friends.

—M.F.A.

A first-time author approaches a book with heightened insecurity, and I am deeply thankful to many people for their inspiration and ideas. I want to thank Max, who is a friend, a tireless visionary, and a gifted storyteller. If one had to write out the quality of stuff that it takes to lead a movement like the MBA Oath, the list of attributes would be long. Max possesses all of these qualities in abundance.

This book is really about the combined passion and conviction of so many MBAs, and I thank them for their inspiration and ideas. Section E, you taught me the most valuable lessons from my MBA experience.

My parents, from the moment I was born in Hawaii, instilled in me a sense of responsibility, curiosity, and the aloha spirit. My four elder siblings—Robin, Chris, Nina, and John—have always blazed a progressive trail, showing me what was possible. Daniel, my one younger sibling, displays energy and generosity. I hope the aggregation of all these traits—responsibility, possibility, and energy—are present in this book and embodied in the MBA Oath movement. Diane, you are my #1 draft pick for a teammate. Thank you for surfing this wave with me.

—P.K.E.

THE MBA OATH

PREAMBLE

As a manager, my purpose is to serve the greater good by bringing together people and resources to create value that no single individual can build alone. Therefore I will seek a course that enhances the value my enterprise can create for society over the long-term. I recognize my decisions can have far-reaching consequences that affect the well-being of individuals inside and outside my enterprise, today and in the future. As I reconcile the interests of different constituencies, I will face difficult choices.

Therefore I promise:

I will act with utmost integrity and pursue my work in an ethical manner. My personal behavior will be an example of integrity, consistent with the values I publicly espouse.

I will safeguard the interests of my shareholders, coworkers, customers, and the society in which we operate. I will endeavor to protect the interests of those who may not have power but whose well-being is contingent on my decisions.

I will manage my enterprise in good faith, guarding against decisions and behavior that advance my own narrow ambitions but harm the enterprise and the people it serves. The pursuit of self-interest is the vital engine of a capitalist economy, but unbridled greed can cause great harm. I will oppose corruption, unfair discrimination, and exploitation.

I will understand and uphold, both in letter and in spirit, the laws and contracts governing my own conduct and that of my enterprise. If I find laws that are unjust, antiquated, or unhelpful I will not brazenly break, ignore, or avoid them; I will seek civil and acceptable means of reforming them.

I will take responsibility for my actions, and I will represent the performance and risks of my enterprise accurately and honestly. My aim will not be to distort the truth but to transparently explain it and help people understand how decisions that affect them are made.

I will develop both myself and other managers under my supervision so that the profession continues to grow and contribute to the well-being of society. I will consult colleagues and others who can help inform my judgment and will continually invest in staying abreast of the evolving knowledge in the field, always remaining open to innovation. I will mentor and look after the education of the next generation of leaders.

I will strive to create sustainable economic, social, and environmental prosperity worldwide. Sustainable prosperity is created when the enterprise produces an output in the long run that is greater than the opportunity cost of all the inputs it consumes.

I will be accountable to my peers and they will be accountable to me for living by this oath. I recognize that my stature and privileges as a professional stem from the respect and trust that the profession as a whole enjoys, and I accept my responsibility for embodying, protecting, and developing the standards of the management profession, so as to enhance that trust and respect.

This oath I make freely, and upon my honor.

Preface

anhattan is generally not considered an earthquake zone. But in 2008, Wall Street suffered nothing short of a high magnitude financial earthquake. Its aftershocks reverberated throughout the world. Afterward, we staggered through the ruins of our 401(k)s, our savings plans, and our retirement dreams, wandering about hollow-eyed and stunned. We clung desperately to our remaining possessions, fearful of stepping into unseen cracks and craters, avoiding the shaming glances of our neighbors, fearful of speaking the truth about what has happened to us and how much we had lost.

In the course of the 2008 economic disaster, the world lost $50 trillion in financial assets, an amount roughly equal to the annual total of the worldwide gross domestic product. The losses brought long-standing, successful companies to their knees. The epicenter was Wall Street, but major financial displacement occurred on Main Street and in nearly every city across the face of the globe. People who worked steadily their entire lives found themselves at the end of their careers, with no job, no pension, and no faith in business. The United States and other governments poured in trillions of dollars to stem the catastrophe, but this approach escalated our national debts to Goliath-sized proportions, a burden that rightfully concerns future generations. The statistics are overwhelming and the numbers are unimaginable, but the human toll of the crisis is real.

We know a man who worked his entire adult life as an estimator in the construction industry. He worked for a large and previously successful company. When the financial catastrophe hit, he lost his job and has been without work for months. At the age of sixty-two, he was not ready for retirement. He had some savings, but they are being depleted. He is a survivor, but he is facing the unknown in the later years of his life without a safety net, without a pension, without a job.

A college buddy, also an MBA, bought a house in California after graduating from business school a couple of years ago. The timing was unfortunate. He bought at the peak of the market and has seen his home value decline to the point where he is now under water on his mortgage. The money he borrowed to pay for the home amounts to more than the worth of the home itself. One in five homeowners in the United States is in the same position.

For many, the pursuit of an MBA is viewed as an opportunity to improve one's career options. Yet, six months after graduation, nearly 10 percent of our classmates at Harvard Business School, supposedly near the top of the MBA food chain, still did not have jobs. This is after investing two years and, in some instances, over $100,000 in tuition and expenses. One classmate said, "I sit in a coffee shop and write cover letters and résumés, trying to maintain a schedule." Another classmate reflected, "My biggest lesson from business school? That you can graduate from Harvard and still be unemployed." The same sentiment is true for graduating students from schools around the world—from Stanford and Wharton to Rensselaer and Thunderbird. It is a time of great uncertainty.

A biblical parable describes a wise man looking for the right foundation on which to build his house. If you take the time to build in the right way, on solid ground, when the storm comes, the house will stand. The storm has come, and apparently our financial house was built upon sand. If we are to rebuild the house, how do we know we are building on a rock or once again building on sandy, shifting soil disguising fault lines? The answers lie in discovering the fault lines beneath the soil, understanding the reasons for their existence, and determining what course of action we should take to prevent or reduce the toll of human suffering should the plates move again.

This book is about the MBA Oath, an initiative we developed to address the crisis we face in business leadership. Our goal is to provoke an examination of these fault lines, the fractures and fissures that cause the great plates of our economy to continually grind against one another, creating instability, disruption, and discontinuity both in business and in private life. Yet, this book is not about the Great Recession but rather a way of conducting business regardless of time and circumstance. In *The MBA Oath,* we present a proposal for a new business ethic. We speak for thousands of our peers who believe that if our generation agrees to conduct their business affairs in accordance with the principles of the oath, we just might have a chance of effecting change for the better. We invite you to consider whether you agree.

This book is written for MBAs—current students, veteran alumni, and prospective students. However, the principles herein are relevant to anyone in business, regardless of their training. We are calling leaders to a new way of doing business, which in reality is simply an affirmation of old-fashioned notions of honesty, trust, and hard work. We want to create a new ethic, a new starting point, and a new way to measure success. The time has come for business to restore its reputation as the friend, not the enemy, of progress in our world.

We have written this book out of our own experience as business school students and now recent MBA graduates. We have had the privilege of helping start and lead the MBA Oath movement along with some very smart and reflective people. Yet the movement is much, much bigger than our individual efforts. Hundreds of students played a role in its genesis. Thousands more are joining ranks. Though our two names appear on the cover of this book, the growth and the development of the oath is the work of many leaders, classmates, professors, and alumni who have inspired us to believe that we can create a better world through business.

We do not intend to preach or evangelize. We intend to make the best argument we can on behalf of the MBA Oath. As you read, you will likely agree with some things and disagree with others. As an adviser to Margaret Thatcher once said, discussions of business values should be an open marketplace, like the world of business is an open marketplace. It should be a forum for debate whose symbol is not the pulpit but the agora of ancient Greece. So read. Debate. Help us find a better way.

The issues that gave rise to this last financial earthquake are still extant. The fault lines run deep. They may very well lie within us, within our own hearts. But we have hope. *The MBA Oath* is premised upon the belief that we *can* manage ourselves, our finances, and our firms in ways that create value without adding unnecessary risk to the system. We *can* earn healthy profits without losing the trust of those who work with us or compete against us. We *can* work with the understanding that we are stewards of a great trust that must be protected. However, whether we *can* do these things and whether we *will* do these things are two very different questions. And whether you are willing to commit to the principles described in this book and apply them to management of your life and business may well make the difference in whether the tremors you feel beneath your feet are positive signs of expanding growth or are the first signs of another great collision of the plates, perhaps even more ferocious than the one through which we are now passing.

The

MBA
OATH

Introduction

In the wake of the worst economic crisis in eighty years, few reputations have endured as severe a beating as those of MBAs. As one writer colorfully put it, "The Masters of Business Administration, that swollen class of jargon-spewing, value-destroying financiers and consultants, have done more than any other group of people to create the economic misery we find ourselves in."[1] Now MBAs are known not just for flashing Power-Point presentations, but also for taking a "greedy, asset-stripping, bubble-inflating approach to management."[2] In the past few years, the term *MBA* has come to stand for either "Mediocre But Arrogant" or "Masters of the Business Apocalypse."

Placing the entirety of blame for the 2008 financial collapse on MBA graduates like us is a bridge too far. On the other hand, holding us blameless is a bridge too short. If two years of full-time professional training does not mean that MBAs will be held to higher standards of ethics and performance, what is the public value of the degree? A 2009 poll highlighted the fact that, by a margin of two to one, the American public had more trust in Congress than in Wall Street for managing the economy.[3] Many speculate that MBA training programs are at best useless and at worst dangerous. We students have felt the sting of such criticism. A classmate wrote how she sees MBAs "cross campus with a slightly defensive hunch of the shoulders, as if expecting to be pelted with rotten tomatoes."[4] Some say that the letters *MBA* on degrees like ours have become scarlet letters of shame.

Even business school professors have joined the chorus of criticism. Shoshana Zuboff, who has spent more than twenty-five years teaching at Harvard Business School, wrote an explosive piece in *BusinessWeek*. "I have come to believe that much of what my colleagues and I taught has caused real suffering, suppressed wealth creation, destabilized the world economy, and accelerated the demise of the twentieth-century capitalism in which the U.S. played the leading role." *Destabilized the world economy? Accelerated the demise of twentieth-century capitalism?* These are serious claims, made all the more striking because they come from someone deep within the business school establishment. "We weren't stupid and we weren't evil," states Zuboff. "Nevertheless we managed to produce a generation of managers and business professionals that is deeply mistrusted and despised by a majority of people in our society and around the world."[5]

Could capitalists actually bring down capitalism? That extreme question seemed ridiculous a few years ago, when economic spirits, housing prices, and leveraged buyouts were flying high.

Giving Up on Business

Not only have many people given up on business schools, many people have given up on business, period. They see news of an accounting scandal on television and they are not surprised because they already expected the worst. A shadow of deep disappointment in business has long been settling upon us. The financial crisis only accelerated the trend. According to one survey, trust in CEOs as spokespeople has dropped to an all-time low of 17 percent in the United States, lower even than the year following the Enron debacle.[6] According the Financial Trust Index, only 10 percent of Americans say they trust large corporations. Contrast that statistic with the fact that forty-five years ago, about 80 percent of U.S. adults said that big business was a "good thing" for the country and thought that business required "little or no change." That latter poll result would be unimaginable today.

You don't need to read the polls, just go to the bookstore or the movies. The very titles chosen for the most popular books that describe the business culture on Wall Street speak volumes: *Barbarians at the Gate, Den of Thieves, Liar's Poker, Fool's Gold.* With the popularity of movies like *Wall Street* and *American Psycho* it is hard to imagine a film portraying a banker in positive light, but sixty years ago, Frank Capra's *It's a Wonderful Life* did just that. In today's cynical climate, the Christmas story of George Bailey, the loyal and conscientious local banker, feels more fictional than Santa Claus.

People are angry and rightly so. Society implicitly trusted business to "do no harm" when it allowed financial markets to operate in a relatively unregulated manner. Now people feel betrayed. If business does not reform itself, government will do the job for it. Some regulation is clearly needed, but if businesspeople remain recalcitrant, resisting all reform, we run the unnecessary risk that even the smallest detail of business life will be dependent upon federal regulation. As political commentator David Gergen put it, "Unless corporate leaders can soon persuade the public to put down their pitchforks, they can expect government to become more and more a master."[7]

The MBA Oath

What if things were different? What if managers thought more highly of their profession? What if instead of insisting that the only social responsibility of business is to maximize profits, they saw themselves as stewards of a trust to create value responsibly? What if we established a professional ethos that gives due recognition to the fact that we are not "Masters of the Universe" but are instead called upon to act as responsible stewards, serving others' interests above our own narrow ambitions? Is it possible to change how we see ourselves and our responsibilities? Is it possible to introduce a new norm in business founded upon the best principles of the past and the best understanding of the present?

In the spring of 2009, on the eve of graduation, a small group of us at Harvard Business School found ourselves staring into a great abyss instead of standing on the threshold of new and exciting careers. We understood that the moment we received our diplomas, regardless of our good intentions and moral foundations, we would be cast in the roles of the Darth Vaders of the business world.

This was not the professional reputation any of us wished to curry as we began our careers. Many of us already had experience in the business world. We understood the realities of the marketplace as well as the public's rightful expectations of business managers. We asked ourselves, "Why is this not working?" The answers we discovered were not surprising. From our perspective, the failures on Wall Street were in the first instance the result of a paucity of vision, a barrenness of soul. The fault lines of the collapse began in the hearts and minds of businesspeople who had lost their way, whose sense of mission and purpose in life had become stunted by fear, greed, and narrow self-interest. The price they and others have paid is still being reckoned. Yet, from our own business education, we knew there were alternatives. We saw beacons of hope in the darkness

One of the most powerful cases we studied in business school was that of James Burke, former CEO of Johnson & Johnson, and how he responded to the discovery that bottles of Tylenol had been tampered with and laced with cyanide. In the fall of 1982, seven individuals in Chicago died from taking normal doses of Tylenol. Burke faced a dire public health risk—how many bottles had been tampered with and what had been done to them? He also faced a serious business risk—Tylenol commanded a 35 percent share of the analgesic market and represented 15 percent of Johnson & Johnson's profits. It was the company's biggest moneymaker. If Johnson & Johnson recalled the medicine, it risked losing the brand forever. Moreover, the authorities concluded that the tampering was limited to Chicago. Burke even received pressure from the head of the FBI to continue selling Tylenol, in order to prevent a widespread public scare. Doing nothing would have been easy. Some thought it would have been wise.

Burke disagreed. He decided to pull every one of the 31 million bottles of Tylenol in America from the shelves, at a cost of $100 million. It was a drastic measure and the consequences were swift. Johnson & Johnson's stock fell seven points in a day. Within a short period, the company's share of the pain reliever market dropped from 35 percent to merely 8. His choice cost the company an enormous amount of money in the short-term. Was it worth it? What about the concept of maximizing shareholder value?

Within days of the crisis, the company aired commercials explaining their actions to regain the public's trust. A few months later, Tylenol was back on the shelves, in an innovative triple tamper-resistant package, the first of its kind. Within six months, the brand had regained its previous market share and had built an unassailable reputation for placing customers first. What brand could be more trusted than one that willingly puts itself at risk for the sake of its customers? Burke's decision to pull Tylenol from the shelves is still widely lauded as one of the great acts of courage in American business history. Why did he do it? Where did he find the resolve to make the decision?

When the Tylenol crisis presented itself, James Burke turned first to Johnson & Johnson's company credo. The credo, which had guided the company for decades, stated in no uncertain terms that the company's number one priority was not hitting its quarterly numbers, but ensuring the health and safety of their customers. The credo was not drafted casually or treated as a dust collector on the back shelves of company headquarters. The credo was a document by which the company abided under Burke's leadership. Johnson & Johnson regularly held "credo challenge meetings" to address the results of the "credo survey," a poll of more than one hundred questions that gave each employee (anonymously) the chance to rate how well the company was living up to the tenets of the credo. In other words, the firm took its principles seriously.[8]

The reason Burke was able to make this decision in the heat of the moment was that *he knew his values ahead of time.* He did not cast about for answers in the midst of the crisis because his values were already in place, and for him the solutions were clear.

Genesis of the MBA Oath

As our class prepared to graduate, a group of us began thinking about what values we stood for—as individuals, as a class, as a school, and as MBAs. The question is not whether or not we have values—everyone has a value system. Every group or organization does as well. The question is whether the values stand the test of moral scrutiny and assessment. Are they the right values or the wrong ones? Peter Drucker, the management guru, said that in times of adversity, in the times "that try a man's soul," values are a necessity. If the right values are absent from a company in such times, he said, "there is no incentive for human beings to walk the extra mile, to make the extra commitment, to do the hard work of rethinking a strategy, of trying new things, of rebuilding. People won't do that just for the money. They will do it only if they believe that what their business does and can do matters. And it is this belief that is instilled by the right values."[9] As individuals and as leaders of firms we ought to ensure our management DNA is of the same quality.

Without a doubt, the financial crisis changed our experience at business school. Companies once thought to be examples of great achievement suddenly failed. Executives once hailed for their business acumen quickly lost their jobs. Financial models once taught as the cutting edge in risk management were abruptly shown to be deeply flawed. If anything good came out of being in business school during the financial crisis, it was that many of us were thrown off our predetermined paths by the rolling uncertainty. Suddenly the solid ground beneath our feet was giving way, and our career plans were either dashed or put on hold. While there was a sense of anxiety on campus, there was also a sense that we were on the verge of an important sea change in business.

There were numerous stories about MBAs in the financial crisis in the months before our graduation. Nearly every story described how MBAs were slimy, self-interested soul suckers who went to the casino with everyone else's money and lost it all when they bet the house. Reading one of these discouraging articles, Max paused and thought—why not challenge our class to take a pledge of business ethics? His wife, Jessica, who studied ethics in graduate school, encouraged him to speak with others in his class. The next day he shared the idea with a classmate, Teal Carlock, at breakfast. His response was immediate and enthusiastic. The two formed a partnership and began nurturing a plan to build a better foundation beneath the teetering walls of the business world, one fashioned upon old-fashioned values of hard work, honesty, and integrity.

At the suggestion of his business ethics professor, Max turned to two Harvard Business School professors, Rakesh Khurana and Nitin Nohria. A week later, Max walked into Rakesh's office in Morgan Hall, which was stacked high with books and disordered in that uniquely professorial way, and announced his desire to formulate a student pledge of ethics at graduation. Rakesh's eyes lit up and a big grin came over his face. He leaped from his chair, bounded to his desk, and exclaimed, "Look at what is on my computer screen right now!" It was a draft of a Hippocratic oath for managers that he and Nitin Nohria had been developing for years and were now working on in conjunction with the World Economic Forum. Rakesh explained that he and Nitin, and the late Professor Sumantra Ghoshal, had been invested in this concept for a very long time but had finally concluded that for the idea to gain real traction, it had to be led by students.

Synchronicity in thought among a variety of people is often a signal that the time and circumstances are ripe for significant change. In Max's mind, the idea was less than twenty-four hours old, but now he was in the presence of a man who had devoted years of his professional life to the concept. Rakesh told Max that major NGOs such as the Aspen Institute and the World Economic Forum were exchanging thoughts and views on the concept. Business associations around the world were exploring the idea. Rakesh was excited. He said, "Let's go find Nitin." They rushed from Rakesh's office, found Professor Nohria, and suddenly everyone was talking all at once.

Both Nitin and Rakesh believed that the oath must proceed from students, not from professors. They insisted it should be formulated, adopted, and advanced through the energy and efforts of those who were about to step into real-world managerial assignments. Nitin and Rakesh wondered how many students would sign on to a student-initiated oath. Max estimated the possibility of one hundred students. The professors were floored. They could not imagine that many students at this late date, barely a few weeks before graduation, would take such an important step at the outset of their business careers. They were delighted and offered to help in any way they could, including encouraging us to use the pledge they had published for the *Harvard Business Review* as a starting point. The professors freely shared their work and offered their expertise and assistance. They became an invaluable source of counsel and inspiration. Their tone of inclusion and sharing imbued the MBA Oath movement with a spirit of cooperation from the beginning.

Max began sharing the idea with others. The response was electric. Whether through word of mouth, Twitter, voice mail, or e-mail, the concept began to alter the usual pregraduation dialogue. Rather than being about where or if people had a job, the conversation turned to what are you going to do once you get a job. Several students from the Kennedy School of Government in the joint-degree program with Harvard Business School (HBS) began to show interest and initiative. Several of them were recipients of the George Fellowship, created by Bill George, the former CEO of Medtronic, a board member of Goldman Sachs, and a pioneer in the concept of integrating public and private service.

Max and others began working tirelessly, putting in long workdays to move the project forward and simultaneously get ready for finals and graduation. He engaged Peter during a dinner one evening at a local haunt and asked him to get on board. Peter, who had been inspired by a class with Professor Khurana in his last semester at HBS, thought, *Why not?* Why not make a stand on how business should be conducted? We might not solve the world's problems, but we could make a commitment to how we wanted to lead in the future. Peter looked at Max squarely and said, "Count me in." Max jumped up from the table, grasping Peter's hand in thanks, and shouted over his shoulder as he ran out the door, "Graduation is in four weeks, Peter. We have to move fast." Peter was left with the rest of his crab cake, and a bewildered look on his face. Time was of the essence.

In early May, we sent the invitation for the first MBA Oath organizing meeting to friends in the graduating class of 2009—friends from all backgrounds, geographies, and industries—consultants, bankers, marketers, private equity professionals from the United States, Mexico, Pakistan, Egypt, and around the world. We met in the student center, Project Room 207. Among the group was Dan Moon, a joint-degree student studying business and medicine; Kate Barton, a former consultant moving to Minnesota to transition her career into brand management; Jon Swan, who cofounded a bank in Colorado; and Rye Barcott, a former Marine who founded an innovative nonprofit to prevent youth violence in a Nairobi slum.

Ten chairs in the room were quickly occupied, and people kept streaming through the door. The room was crackling with energy. People were coming not out of curiosity but because they wanted to be part of something that would make a difference. Soon there were too many people and not enough space. You could feel the excitement. The last to arrive stood for an entire ninety minutes just outside the door because the room had filled to capacity. The purpose of the meeting was to present, discuss, and finalize a draft of a Hippocratic oath for business and get our classmates to sign. How could we get it done in a month? None of us had ever launched a student movement before. We had no idea that what we were about to do would soon reverberate not only across our country but in more than fifty countries around the world. At the time, we were simply focused on our own graduating class at Harvard.

Using the oath drafted by Professors Nohria and Khurana as a starting point, we began to craft our own version. We compared it to other oaths and pledges: the Hippocratic oath for doctors, legal oaths, even the presidential oath. We reviewed promises and pledges from forward-thinking business schools such as Thunderbird, Columbia, and Dartmouth. We researched international standards such as the Global Standards Codex and the Principles of Responsible Management Education. We sought to take the best of current business thought and ethics and incorporate the core values into our oath. After a great deal of discussion, debate, and, frankly, hollering, groaning, cheering, and laughing, we finished a product that seemed right to most. We called it the MBA Oath.

After that meeting, things really began heating up. We did not have a lot of resources, but we were scrappy. While on a short trip with his wife and daughter, Max built a simple Web site where students could learn about the oath and officially sign it online. Teal Carlock led the organizing effort on campus. Classmates began signing the oath online. Word started leaking to other schools. There was a buzz that this could become something special. As graduation approached, Max received a call from a reporter. Leslie Wayne of the *New York Times* wanted to know more about the oath. The following day the story of the MBA Oath appeared on the front page of the business section of the *Times*. It garnered an amazing amount of commentary in blog posts and Internet exchanges. The story fired up discussions across the globe. Soon afterward, a number of other media outlets wanted to cover the MBA Oath: *BusinessWeek*, the *Financial Times*, the *Economist, NPR*. Then students from other business schools contacted us, asking how they could join the movement. We knew we were hitting a central cultural vein when *The Daily Show* did a piece on the movement, poking fun at the students who *did not* sign it.

While the media attention was positive, the team was focused on another urgent issue—putting together an oath-signing ceremony for Class Day in June, the day prior to graduation. This would be the first formal public announcement of the MBA Oath. This would also be our first outward, visible step toward peer accountability. In a moving ceremony the day before graduation, several hundred Harvard Business School students stood together in Burden Auditorium to publicly take the oath.

Nearly two-thirds of our graduating class at Harvard Business School signed the oath, six times the number we had estimated. The truth is that the response we received, both at Harvard and around the world, was unexpected and overwhelming. We do not think the response we have garnered is due to our team's genius launch strategy, or even the content of the oath itself. Rather, in the aftermath of the financial meltdown, the world was groaning for change. We stepped forward with an idea. We are pushing for a new ethic, a new responsibility, a new mission. The oath is a call to duty, a call for change, and a call for renewal in the way we do business, in the way we envision the role of business in society.

In 2010, U.S. schools will award more than 150,000 MBA degrees, more than twice the number of law degrees and medical degrees combined. But an MBA degree does not make you a "professional." What if it did? What if MBAs, upon their graduation, committed to holding themselves to a higher standard of self-regulation? What if business schools taught and advanced a code of conduct, a set of norms establishing standards of ethical competence among business managers and owners, the management equivalent of the Hippocratic oath? What if we MBAs actually lived up to our billing and became leaders who don't just make a difference *in* the world, but make a difference *for* the world? That is the future we want to see. That is the future envisioned and embraced by the MBA Oath.

THE PROFESSION

THE TROUBLE WITH
BUSINESS SCHOOLS

Being an MBA means strongly committing to building
something new, to competing with others while respecting
the rules of the game and respecting the people we lead.

Paolo Mazza, MIP Business School—
Politecnico di Milano, Italy, Class of 2009, signer #1408

When you walk into a doctor's office you are likely
to see a medical license and degree framed on the
office wall. Although you probably do not consciously
think about it, those framed documents convey a message: *You
can trust this person.* You expect that your doctor is there to help
you. You assume, for better or worse, that he has your best interests in mind. Your problems are being handled by a person who is
professionally committed to doing the right thing. Why is it that
when you see a framed MBA diploma, you do not get the same
feeling?

What if an MBA conveyed a message of reassurance that
the holder of the degree was committed to honesty, integrity,
industriousness, and commitment to the common good? What
if MBAs were known more for their wisdom rather than their

recklessness, their humility rather than their egos, their honesty rather than their guile? What if having an MBA actually meant that you held certain principles of professional behavior from which you would not waver? What if you walked into a business-person's office and were actually relieved when you saw an MBA degree on the wall?

───────

We want to state plainly that we are fans of business education. We count the two years we spent in business school among the best of our lives. We worked harder than we thought we could, learned more than we expected, and made deeper friendships than we would have anticipated. We have no doubt that our training and our degrees are of great professional value. We think it was an invest-ment well made for the long-term. On the other hand, we recog-nize that our education was not without its own troubles, the most interesting of which are rarely discussed in the business press.

The truth is that the MBA is a degree that needs to be redefined. Today, no one knows what it really means. Among business schools there is no common body of knowledge mastered by students, no agreed-upon number of credit hours required, and no formal licensures offered. You can earn an MBA in a one-year program or in two years, part-time or full-time, in person or online. Such flex-ibility is great, but what does it say about substance and content? Today more than *ten thousand* institutions around the world grant MBA degrees. Of those institutions, which ones are producing committed, serious graduates conscious not only of their income potential but also of their public responsibilities and duties?

Although the MBA Oath is not about reforming business edu-cation writ large, we developed it in response to our education.

Giving a picture of the questions we encountered in our studies is a way of setting the stage for the unfolding drama of the formation of the oath. In this and the next two chapters we explore what MBA education is like in the present, what it meant in the past, and what we think it ought to mean in the future.

In our business school's campus library, a tablet describes the institution's vision *"to promote knowledge and integrity in the art of finance, industry and commerce."* If that simple and clear vision were realized, and business school graduates were known for knowledge and integrity, the entire field of management would be transformed. For many of our classmates, this vision statement defined their aspirations. Somewhere along the way though, many of us lose sight of why we are there. Though the vision is etched in stone, the friction of business school culture can rub the vision away and bury it among the stacks' past business cases.

This is the trouble with business schools, that *without intending to do so*, they contribute to the Great Forgetfulness of who you are and what you stand for. The consequence of the forgetfulness is that graduates may leave school less prepared than they could be to lead people and organizations effectively. We could write much on this subject, but we will limit ourselves to four areas to illustrate the point: privilege, rankings, compartmentalization, and ethics.

Privilege—A Trip to the Chocolate Factory

When we applied to business school, we wanted to enlarge our skill sets, develop leadership abilities, and open professional doors for ourselves. We nursed an idea that we wanted to make a difference in the world, but we were not sure what that would be. Whatever we did, we held a vague notion that, once we got into business school, we would be able to do "whatever we wanted to do."

When we got our phone calls saying we had been admitted to Harvard Business School, we felt like the children who won golden tickets to Willy Wonka's chocolate factory. The guided tour confirmed the place to be as fantastic as we had imagined. True, we did not discover rivers of chocolate or edible marsh-mallow pillows, but the campus held other wonders. The gym features world-class art displayed on walls of dark wood and rich red-leather panels. The cafeteria boasts of multiple full-time sushi chefs. The campus is guarded by a veritable army of groundskeepers. They say that in autumn a leaf falling from a tree never touches the grass because the grounds crew catches it in mid-air. The unspoken message of these amenities is that this is a place of privilege; indulge yourself.

Attending a prestigious business school is in some ways akin to getting a country club membership. The dues are expensive, but the cachet of having membership in an elite and well-heeled fra-ternity is an end in itself. Some students, particularly those com-ing directly from finance and consulting, view business school as a two-year vacation from the eighty-hour workweeks. Finally, they have a few hours to golf, travel, and even enjoy life. They now have the opportunity to relive freshman year of college, this time with more expensive beer.

Harvard Business School, like many business schools, requires a six-figure tuition commitment over the course of two years. Most students cannot afford to pay cash, so we take out loans to finance our education. For graduate students of other disciplines, such as education, sociology, medicine, and social work, the looming threat of future loan payments causes them to live modestly while in school. Not so in the business school culture. Most Harvard MBA students don't eat macaroni and cheese at home to save money. The campus culture subtly and not so subtly encourages students to spend expensive nights out at bars and restaurants and to experience exotic vacations around the world. The silent social curriculum urges students to conform to privilege and self-indulgence.

The oft-repeated justification is that future earnings will quickly repay student loans and extensions of credit. To keep pace, most students rely upon debt. In other words, we learn to spend money we don't have because the "value" game at business school has more to do with one's net worth or *perceived* net worth than with the value one's services might add to the larger community. It is less about what you can give and more about what you can get.

MBAs learn about juicing returns with debt in finance class, but it is outside of class that students learn the power of credit. By taking out the maximum amount in loans (and in many cases by opening a few no-interest-for-one-year credit cards), MBA students learn that debt is a way to "juice" our lifestyles as well. Taking on as much debt as they can, MBA grads assume that they will be able to pay off the loans later. These choices, however, come with second-order consequences. Graduating from an elite business school with a $150,000 debt, students have little choice except to seek out the high-finance big-bonus path.[1]

When MBA graduates leave school, is it any wonder they often seek to "lever up" their companies with debt to secure extra performance? They have been trained to operate this way in their personal lives during business school. Why not apply the same debt principle to their firms? Business school may be where you can find the cleverest uses of credit, but it is unlikely to be the place you will find the wisest uses of it.

Rankings—A Trip to the Newsstand

Among the most powerful shapers of public opinion on the quality and content of business education are the periodicals that annually rank business schools—*U.S. News & World Report*, the *Wall Street Journal*, the *Economist*, the *Financial Times*. We admit it; we both looked carefully at the rankings when we applied to business school. Everyone does—both students and adminstrators. In these assessments, journalists rank the "top ten" or "top twenty-five" schools. What do they mean when they say that a school has been rated as a top-tier school? What factors do they consider in their rankings?

A school's ranking is greatly influenced by a single metric: What is the average compensation of graduates during their first year after business school? The larger the average salaries of the business school graduates, the higher the school will be ranked. Arguably, the "proof of the pudding is in the eating," and business schools are about making money, so why not? However, that conclusion presupposes that business pudding is only about cash received, not about services rendered. The metrics are skewed in favor of values obtained, not values added.

The ranking system is reasonable on its face. School is expensive and if students choose to attend, they want to know their expected return on investment. But what starts as a reasonable system degrades quickly into a narrow focus on a single number. The failure to perceive this fault line leads the rankers to examine the wrong data in assessing the quality of the educational experience. By skewing the rankings to favor those schools producing the highest moneymakers in the first year out of school, journalists become complicit in the denial system that the MBA is about anything other than personal self-advancement.

Imagine a core course curriculum structured to inspire superior business leadership for the good of the public as well as for the long-term viability of the corporation. Many suggest that these are not inconsistent goals but are in fact entirely consistent. Recent economic history demonstrates they are correct.

When a business school markets itself through advertising ploys such as, "You will increase your salary by 50% by coming to our school!" they are pandering to a certain type of student, one focused primarily on personal financial wealth. When business school rankings are premised on first-year postgraduation salaries, the "best and the brightest" are invited to conform to the wealth-acquisition mindset. The message is that if you want to be number one, you do so because you are expected to make more money than anyone else. This is the hype that entices students to the school. Instead of producing a generation of public-spirited leaders whose gifts may be utilized to lift the spirit of a nation, the enterprise of such schools is almost exclusively oriented around the acquisition of personal wealth. Thus, compensation, not value, is the keystone of the education.

The rankings game passes through the social life of students, who are imbued from their first day on campus with the social pressure of landing a big job or internship. At times, business school can feel like little more than a two-year-long networking night, a place to make professional connections. Many students carry smartly designed business cards. We fuss and preen before every campus recruiter, every professor, and even among classmates, seeking not wisdom or thoughtful conversation but instead potential job leads. We are, however, living in a new era when self-advancement alone has proved to be a dangerous managerial mindset. The challenge to business schools and new MBA graduates is to think not only in terms of personal profit incentives but also in terms of the larger social impact of one's decisions and sustaining a long-term rather than short-term vision of value and reward. The MBA degree must become a signification of who you are in your heart, not just a name tag on your lapel.

Business schools must learn to adjust their sights beyond the next year's rankings. They must commit themselves not simply to excellence in teaching functional skill sets but also in teaching and inspiring moral leadership and courage. There *are* alternatives. The Aspen Institute publishes its own ranking of business schools, *Beyond Grey Pinstripes,* which considers the leadership development and ethical components of the education. Former Yale School of Management dean Joel Podolny proposes another solution: the AACSB, which is the business school accreditation body, could take leadership. They could "delegitimize such rankings by prescribing, and auditing, how the schools use the data in their communications. For instance, it could forbid business schools from touting in their advertising how much their degrees will augment graduates' incomes. The AACSB could also insist on compliance as a criterion for accreditation. The rankings would still be available to potential applicants through the media, but the official guidelines could force business schools to articulate their goals in ways that do not boil down to a single number."[2] No solution is perfect, then again, neither is the current situation.

Compartmentalization

Another area of trouble in business education is the compartmentalization of the curriculum. Business leaders should be taught to continually strive to see the big picture, but in our experience, the curriculum was offered up in narrow slices. Though a hefty smorgasbord of course offerings was on the table, ranging from economics to operations to finance, rarely were we encouraged to seek a unifying theme among our courses. We understand that this is now changing at our alma mater and at some other schools. This is a good thing.

Management education for the most part is subdivided into functional silos, separate stores of knowledge from which one draws disparate bits of information. One silo may be marketing, another finance, another accounting, and so on. At Harvard, the professors utilize the case method of teaching, discussing the particular decisions made and results obtained in specific cases and decisions faced by real business leaders. They tend to select the cases solely based on what they may reveal about a marketing, financing, or accounting strategy. In other words, the discussion about any given case is limited to a particular functional perspective. Again, though this serves to equip students with dandy tools to hang from their tool-belt, the lessons to be learned are too often limited to functionality rather than long-term purpose. The risk in this approach is that new managers are taught they only need to think of their responsibilities in a functionally narrow manner. They are not taught to think integratively, how these decisions may affect larger pools of interest or serve the common welfare.

As one commentator stated, "Aspiring business leaders are often trained as compartmentalized clinicians rather than whole persons who assess both the analytical and social implications of business decisions. In the pursuit of rigor, a corresponding and unintended depersonalization process has occurred. A student's ability to hedge currency risk may have greater value than engaging in honest conversation about *doing the right thing*."[3] In such a compartmentalized academic environment, students are invited to focus on the "hard" courses, like finance, rather than the "soft" courses, like leadership and ethics. Schools of course do not encourage this, but simply separating a course on ethics or leadership from the rest of the curriculum signals that the course is more a standalone discipline than a foundation for the rest of the curriculum.

We remember studying a case on outsourcing manufacturing to East Asia. A student suggested that one risk of such outsourcing is being complicit in supporting sweatshops. The professor instructed the class to "hold comments like that" because this was a case about *strategy*, not ethics. But is that not itself a myopic view of strategy? If a company is not sensitive to the strategic risks imposed by the ethics of its actions, it will be blindsided by consumers who demand more of the firm.

Perhaps we would be better off under a system like that proposed by Joel Podolny, who argues for structuring teaching teams "where faculty from both 'hard' and 'soft' disciplines develop material and present it in the same classroom." If that were to happen, students would be challenged to undo their assumptions that finance is a "hard" course and ethics or leadership is a "soft" course. The curriculums would be integrated in order that one discipline would always be available to inform the other.[4] In a compartmentalized curriculum, we forget to perceive and appreciate the human fault lines, which may translate to real-life economic and social ruptures of devastating magnitude. We neglect the things we once knew, that the fault lines lay between the silos of knowledge, standing alone, disconnected and inattentive to other stores of wisdom.

Ethics

We asked student body presidents at seven of the world's top business schools about their school's ethics courses—the responses varied widely, from a short four-week curriculum in the first year to optional electives. These were anecdotes, but there was a clear theme: many business schools give insubstantial attention to business ethics. If moral leadership and moral self-examination are not taught in business school, we might as well strike our colors and abandon ship. Theodore Roosevelt stated that to educate a person in mind and not in morals is to educate a menace to society. Thankfully, a movement is afoot at business schools to add courses studying not only the financial crisis but also ethics. The number of freestanding ethics courses at MBA programs has grown by five times since 1988. But adding a business ethics course does not guarantee a robust ethics curriculum. Casually discussing ethics in the abstract where no one is committing real dollars or withholding real dollars from a real-life situation can be viewed as a "soft" course without significant personal consequence other than its impact on a student's overall GPA.

Business ethics must be taught by the most gifted and insightful professors. If such courses are dismissed as touchy-feely or "light," students will likewise treat course content as so much expensive frosting added to their education. A learned, respected, and wise professor, however, can invest such courses with energy and fire, provoking searing debate and fostering both intensity and passion in the students. We have seen such professors at work. That type of instruction is not only engaging, it is inspirational, and it is effective. We were lucky to have such instructors. We have already forgotten a variety of financial formulas we were taught in business school, but we will never forget the fierce conversations sparked by our ethics course.

Ethical instruction should not be limited to one course. Neither should it be relegated to the marginal fringe of elective courses in the curriculum. Business ethics and professional responsibility should be woven like a bright thread throughout the tapestry of business education. The moral consequences of one's business decisions should be a consistent theme visited daily in the business school curriculum. The notion must be encouraged that it is impossible to do the bread-and-butter work of business without consciously considering values and ethics.

The case method of instruction is a helpful tool for giving students self-awareness because it forces students to think through how they would make decisions if they were to step into the shoes of the case protagonist. It may be as close as you can come to creating real leadership tests in a classroom. The danger of the case method, however, is that if the instructor functions solely as a facilitator and not a wisdom leader, the students are not challenged to think beyond their own emotional and intellectual boundaries.

A gifted business professor will not simply encourage cross talk among the students (a convenient way to eat up an hour of time) but will also probe and provoke discussion in areas of discomfort and ambiguity. At times, professors must profess, not merely facilitate. As Barry Mitnick has written, "Self-training, like self-medication, is best done under professional direction."[5] Perhaps the territory you propose to explore is beyond the personal experience of a particular professor. What then? In that case, the professor as well becomes a student and fearlessly admits what he or she does not know and invites discussion leading toward deeper understanding by all. The etymological roots of the word *educate* come from the Latin word *educere*, meaning "to lead forth." Thus, education itself should be an exercise in leadership, not simply an exercise in learned sibling rivalry. The professor must at some point lead by example and show the way. A wise person knows the importance of understanding not only what is known but also what is not known, including invisible fault lines that may some day lead to calamitous human events.

Certain professors have a knack for accomplishing this goal. They have a way of hitting the high notes of human experience and leading students toward compassion as well as excellence and commitment. Our marketing professor Youngme Moon was impossibly upbeat and prepared and pointed us, and our classmates, to deeper ideas of leadership and human understanding. In class, she discussed how her baby awoke with a fever and how she tried to treat the fever with a branded infant medication. At first the fever continued to rise. Frantic for help, my professor called her sister as well as the child's pediatrician. Both advised her to remain calm and trust the medication to work. After repeated calls and repeated reassurances, the child's fever broke.

Moon called this an "oxygen moment," a moment when she could again breathe free with clarity and relief. As a new parent, she feared the worst but was forced by circumstance into a trust relationship with a pharmaceutical manufacturer. She was leery of placing her trust there, but with the encouragement of the physician and her sister, she regained her composure, calmly acquiesced to the advice she was given, and stepped into a silent trust partnership with a large pharmaceutical company to care for her son. The partnership succeeded.

Moon used the story to emphasize to our class that what we do in business *matters*. Marketing is not simply a strategy for selling more units. It also implies the formation of trust relationships between companies and customers, at times involving matters of life and death.

We are not suggesting that MBA programs can transform a twenty-five-year-old's values in a matter of two years. Students enter business school with value systems built over the course of a lifetime. Many enter business school with little or no interest in reshaping those values. On the other hand, we all have gaps or blind spots in our moral and ethical perspectives. Therein we may discover the hidden fault lines that can be exploited by others as we move through difficult life passages. To the extent a business school education demands that we become aware of those blind spots, we are so much better prepared for identifying and averting potential disasters down the road. Ethics classes in business education ought to attempt to do four things: enable students to recognize ethical dilemmas; broaden the student's range of response; teach tools for action; and test the consistency of student's beliefs, forcing them to become more self-aware by examining their own beliefs.

At some schools, this project is already under way. Robert Bruner, the dean of the Darden School of Business at the University of Virginia, extols the virtues of having a university-wide honor system. "At Darden, ethics isn't just a course title; it is a core belief in creating value that has good societal implications as opposed to mere economic outcomes . . . We give a required and graded course in business ethics, but ethics is also a part of the regular conversation in many courses and co-curricular activities. Moreover, for the community to have any moral suasion, the oath must be a condition of membership in the community. One's choice should be whether or not to join the community, not whether or not to take the oath. At the University of Virginia, agreeing to abide by the honor system is a condition of admission."[6] Tuck School of Business at Dartmouth also has a broad honor code and allows its MBA students to take exams home to write, rather than sequestering them in a room supervised by watchful monitors. Creating an environment of trust creates greater freedom and reinforces the incentives to play by the rules.

Perhaps more thought should be given to emphasizing ethics and character as requirements for admission to business schools. In selecting candidates for the MBA degree, business schools signal that they are satisfied the potential degree recipient is competent to run an organization, whether it be for profit or nonprofit. To what extent do business school admissions programs emphasize the importance of character and honesty in selecting a pool of potential first-year students? All business school applicants should be required to write essays setting forth their personal ethical statements. From whom did they learn their value system? What do they deem to be the most important features of their own ethical codes of conduct? Business school admissions committees should assume responsibility for selecting candidates who will possess not only excellent technical skills but also moral courage.

———

Read the admissions essays of incoming MBAs and you will come across moving descriptions of how they want to live their lives and use their skills to make a contribution to the world through their work. The cynical might say that these essays are mere marketing collateral, less representative of the truth than of the applicants' intense desire to get into their school of choice by saying whatever they think will tickle the ears of the admissions committee. No doubt, this is true for some, but we disagree it is the case for most. Having gone through the process ourselves, the work of putting pen to paper to talk about our strengths and weaknesses, our most substantial accomplishments, what we have learned from our mistakes, and what our career visions are is a difficult task, requiring a great degree of self-reflection.

Law schools and medical schools depend far more upon standardized tests than on essays to select their students. For business schools, the essay may be the most important section of the application. It gives reviewers a sense of who the students are, what they care about, and what they want to do with their education. For applicants, it forces us to crystallize the vague thoughts we have about ourselves and what we want to do with our lives. Not everyone writes about saving the world, but the best essayists are those who combine pragmatic realism with a broader vision for how they can make a difference. The process is enlightening and causes you to begin your business education with a sense of purpose. Business school, though, has a way of distracting you from that purpose. It can cause you to forget your own higher aspirations.

The MBA Oath calls us to remember what we are tempted to forget as business students. It is a reminder that our purpose is not to lead lives of privilege. Our reason for being is not to rise in social rankings. Our calling is not to become compartmentalized clinicians. The themes of the oath are the themes of our application essays—integrity, service, impact.

The oath is a reminder also of the original intent of management education. When business schools were first founded, the institutional entrepreneurs who created them were inspired by a vision of changing the way business was practiced at a fundamental level. Their vision for business management is radically different from the status quo today. It was to build toward a future when you could walk into a businessperson's office, see an MBA on the wall, and it would give you as much reassurance as if you had seen a medical degree. Their vision was to make management a profession. It is to that founding vision that we now turn.

THE GREAT, BUT DELICATE EXPERIMENT

As an MD/MBA student who has already taken the Hippocratic oath, why will I take the MBA Oath? Medicine ranks among the noblest of professions due to a practitioner's dedication to their patients. I see no reason why business managers cannot be just as dedicated to creating value for society.

Dan Moon, Columbia Medical School/
Harvard Business School, Class of 2009, signer #266

In 1908, when Harvard began the world's first two-year masters program in management education, it was called a "great, but delicate experiment," by Lawrence Lowell, who would go on to become president of the University. The experiment proposed to turn the occupation of management into a profession, like law or medicine, where members of the profession would act with the public good in mind. Leaders of the business school movement wanted to ensure that large corporations, which were just coming into existence, would be operated in the interests of society. In essence, they made an effort to say, "We are all in this together."

The question is, *Has the great but delicate experiment succeeded?* Is society better off for having MBAs? The notion of an MBA graduate being committed to the greater good of society almost sounds preposterous. Yet improving society was exactly what business schools were originally intended to do.

When you think about it, the advent of the business school era happened rather suddenly. For several thousand years, the world had gotten along very well without business schools. Then, all of a sudden, they began popping into existence at the beginning of the twentieth century. Within a hundred years, the number of institutions granting MBAs grew from zero to roughly ten thousand. What happened? And what was the purpose? Who needed an MBA anyway?

The truth is, formally organized business corporations are a relatively recent invention. Less than 150 years ago, even in the most advanced nations of the world, most people had little or no contact with large businesses. They just did not exist. In fact, outside of government and religious institutions, few large organizations of any kind existed. Even medium-sized businesses were rare. Most people worked on their farms, or if they were more commercially engaged, they worked in small businesses. Toward the close of the nineteenth century, things began to shift in the United States. Large corporations like U.S. Steel and Standard Oil gained ascendance and began employing thousands. The challenge was to effectively manage all of these people across space and time. Slowly society began changing; more people began working outside of their homes, as parts of sprawling organizations. Perceptive observers recognized that these new large business organizations would change the social order in profound and unpredictable ways. What could be done to ensure these new entities would do more good than harm?

At the beginning of the twentieth century, an entrepreneurial group of business leaders and academics responded to these concerns by proposing to create university-based graduate business schools. The idea of creating business schools was to ensure that large corporations would serve the interests of society by transforming the occupation of management into a bona fide profession. Founders of business schools believed that large commercial organizations should be led by managers who subscribed to a professional ethic emphasizing stewardship of the public trust. "When their graduates managed companies," explains business school historian Rakesh Khurana, "it was supposed to result in more than just the creation of private wealth. In fact, the schools wanted to create a new class of leaders, who would play a service role in industrial society."

When Harvard Business School opened its campus in 1908, Owen Young, the president of General Electric, addressed the crowd. His words give a picture of the school's mission to train students in a new profession:

> Today the *profession* of business at Harvard formally makes its bow to its older brothers and holds its head high with the faith of youth. Today we light the fires in the temple which it is the trust of Harvard to maintain and from which may be renewed through generation after generation the high ideals, the sound principles, the glorious traditions, which makes a *profession*. Today and here business formally assumes the obligations of a *profession*, which means responsible action as a group, devotion to its own ideals, the creation of its own codes, the capacity for its honors, and the responsibility for its own discipline, the awards of its own service.[1] [italics added for emphasis]

What Owen Young put into words was the general consensus concerning the founding of the world's first graduate business schools: business leaders should be trained with a professional ethos to manage their organizations prudently, both for their shareholders and for the benefit of society. Far from being asset-stripping, greed-dominated opportunists, graduate students in management were to become professionals with deep responsibilities. They were to promote a capitalism for the common good.

Even today, the mission statements of many of the world's leading business schools indicate that they view their mission as far broader than simply teaching students how to make a buck. Harvard aims to "educate leaders who *make a difference in the world.*" MIT Sloan attempts to "develop *principled*, innovative leaders who improve the world." Virginia's Darden School commits to "*improve society* by developing leaders in the world of practical affairs." Stanford's mission is to "develop innovative, *principled*, and insightful leaders who *change the world.*" The hard-nosed, traditionally finance-heavy Wharton School defines its mission as preparing "business leaders who fuel the growth of industries and economies," but then amplifies on this mission statement on its Web site, where it declares, "When you lead with inspiration and deep knowledge, you won't just advance your own goals, you'll *advance society* as well."[2]

A gap exists, however, between the stated goals of the schools and the outcomes they produce. The Aspen Institute recently completed a study of how business schools influence the attitudes and behavior of their graduates. They found that rather than instilling students with the notion that they have professional responsibilities, the opposite has occurred. Surveying a large number of MBA graduates from a broad range of business schools, the Institute inquired what the graduates believed to be the purpose of a business corporation. The survey revealed that before obtaining an MBA degree, students believed the purpose of a corporation was to develop goods and services for the benefit of society. Upon graduation, however, the students declared that the purpose of a corporation was to maximize shareholder value.

Maximizing shareholder value is not immoral, inappropriate, or unjustifiable. In fact, it is a *good* goal, even a noble goal. But, as we will argue in this book, maximizing shareholder profits is not the *only* goal of a business or corporation. The Aspen Institute survey demonstrates a serious disconnect between the educational goals of the recipients of business degrees and the stated goals of the institutions conferring the degrees. The apparent goals of the degree recipients, moreover, are far removed from the vision of the founding leaders of the business school curriculum.

Compare our experience to that of James Burke, the legendary former Johnson & Johnson CEO, who attended Harvard Business School in the late 1940s. "In everything we did," he recalls, "we were reminded of the moral values—the importance of the moral values in our decision making. We all spent a lot of time talking about it." At the time of Burke's attendance, the school wrote that its educational policy was designed to help students develop the beginnings of an *integrated social and economic philosophy*. This included the understanding of ethical considerations as an integral part of business administration.[3]

Though we share the same degree from the same institution as James Burke, one might question whether we received the same education. Our experience was intense and exciting from the standpoint of state-of-the-art technical instruction, but Mr. Burke received his education in the context of the rich tapestry of human experience and moral choice. One must wonder whether the lessons he learned in his business education helped enable him to face the Tylenol crisis so well. One wonders if our generation will be as well equipped. What happened to the great, but delicate experiment?

A large part of the answer can be traced to the business school reforms post–World War II. In the 1950s, around the fiftieth anniversary of the founding of the first business schools, the Ford Foundation and the Carnegie Corporation each published independent studies on the quality and effectiveness of management education. Neither report was complimentary. They found that after World War II, as America rapidly industrialized and demand for managers grew, a number of universities launched business schools to meet the growing demand for business school graduates. Many of the schools were neither well conceived nor well managed. As a result, the poor quality of the faculty, research, curriculum, and students was deemed "indefensible."[4]

The reports stated that the level of instruction and scholarship was atrocious. They concluded that business schools were led by pseudo-academics who had not been vetted by the same rigorous standards used to evaluate professors in more traditional disciplines like economics, engineering, and statistics. The report's authors recommended that business schools could improve the strength and rigor of their academic programs if they reseeded their faculties with more quantitatively focused instructors. Then they put their money where their mouths were. The Ford Foundation itself invested $175 million to modernize and improve the MBA degree, resulting in the basic educational model we recognize today. Within five years, business school faculties were specialized along traditional academic lines, placing particular emphasis on economics and quantitative analysis.

Business education had changed. The reforms achieved their goals in many ways. The acadmic standards got tougher. But there was a tradeoff. The purpose of business schools changed. It was no longer to turn management into a profession; it was to turn management into a science. Business professors became more like academics in other disciplines, researching increasingly narrow and obscure areas so they could publish and win the esteem of their peers. The focus on training leaders who could competently and responsibly manage complex organizations was almost lost in a new age of training analysts with the newest financial formulas. The "great, but delicate experiment" of turning management into a profession had ended.

———

We say it is time to begin the experiment anew. The MBA Oath is a call to return to the roots of why business schools were formed. The vision of those who originally founded business schools was not only noble, but splendid. Our best chance of creating sustainable wealth and hope among the people of this nation and nations around the globe is to augment our modern-day sophisticated business skills with the timeless principles of the past. We need to move from an ethos of excuses and self-justification to one of social and communal accountability. We need to shift from a culture of timid acquiescence to one of responsibility and interdependence.

It is time to change and a professional oath is an appropriate place to begin. Sociologist Robert K. Merton argued that codes have enormous influence on behavior because they provide guidelines. They can produce negative emotions of shame when the code is broken or positive feelings of pride when it is kept. As

sociologists have long known, these emotions are powerful moti-
vators, often more powerful than material rewards. For example:
"I can't do that. I'm a doctor!" Or "I won't do that. I'm a judge."
What if you heard someone say, "I won't do that. I'm an MBA."

The fact is, businesspeople are still expected to act with professional selflessness at times, to not engage in insider-trading, to
avoid conflicts of interest, to honor their contracts, and to treat
employees fairly. Were it otherwise we would shrug our shoulders and say, "business as usual." But the fact is we *are* shocked
and we *are* disappointed when we hear about investment bankers
squandering money in pursuit of short-term profits or corporate
executives utilizing government bailout money to decorate plush
office quarters. Our disappointment implies that we have higher
hopes for business leaders. You cannot be both disappointed in
such behavior and simultaneously argue that business leaders
and managers have no responsibility to the larger society.

Given that we already have expectations of business leaders,
and that those expectations are reasonable, the question becomes
how business leaders can meet the expectations we place upon
them. To answer this, it is worth returning to the founding vision
of business schools to make management a profession. What does
it mean to be a professional anyway?

Angel Cabrera, the dean of Thunderbird, the first U.S. business school with a mandatory professional oath, comments that
a profession "can be seen as the diligent application of specialized knowledge for the resolution of complex problems of great
social consequence."[5] Doctors apply special knowledge to complex problems of health. Engineers apply special knowledge to
complex problems of building safe structures like bridges. Lawyers apply special knowledge to complex problems of jurispru-
dence. Because of this special mission, members of a profession

enter into an implicit social contract with society. In every case, the problems addressed by professionals are of great social consequence. We need them done right. The professional person, as the adage goes, does not work in order to be paid, but is paid in order to work.

We do not tend to think of business and the field of management as satisfying these criteria, but we should revisit our assumptions. Business managers create, shape, and influence the lives and incomes of nearly every person on the planet. This was not so two hundred years ago, but it is undeniable today. Given such far-reaching influence, business schools and business professors have not only the opportunity but also the obligation to ensure that business students understand the grave and weighty responsibilities they assume when they engage in local and global commercial activities.

An occupation only earns the right to be a profession when some ideals that go beyond following the law become an integral part of the conduct of the people in that field. Judged by that standard, some businesspeople conduct themselves like professionals, but management as a whole could not be considered a profession. However, as we have seen, business schools were initially created to train professionals. Even if they fail in that duty today, we should not confuse what *is* with what *should be.* Joel Podolny has written that business schools today are basically trade schools. "There's nothing wrong with trade schools," Podolny says, "but, since MBAs occupy positions with enormous responsibility that have a huge impact on society, their ability to do harm is very great—greater than the damage that people trained in trade schools can cause."[6]

Four hallmark features characterize professions. First, professions establish a code of conduct that governs the behavior of their members. The code establishes voluntary constraints on the actions of the members that do not necessarily follow the dictates of the market. Doctors in emergency rooms may be required to serve those who cannot afford their services (a drain on profitability). Lawyers may be constrained from discussing the truth of what they know because of the attorney-client privilege (despite the public's clamor for information). As two of our mentors, Rakesh Khurana and Nitin Nohria, explain, in return for receiving society's trust for their occupational category, professions promise that their members are worthy of the trust. "Professions perform the social function of defining and enforcing a set of values and norms that counter the purely self-interested logic of markets. . . . It is a way of imparting to members a body of socially valuable knowledge and skills as well as a set of attitudes about how they should use their knowledge and skills."[7]

Second, professions enforce the codes through a governing body of respected peers who ensure compliance. For example, doctors can lose their licenses and lawyers can be disbarred. Third, professions require members to demonstrate mastery of a codified body of knowledge—doctors must pass their board exams, and lawyers must pass the bar. Fourth, professions require members to continue their education throughout their careers and stay abreast of the evolving knowledge in their field. In the law, continuing legal education requirements include a mandatory number of ethics credits within the course of each compliance period.

Based on these criteria, the great, but delicate experiment has not succeeded. Management is not a profession, and the MBA is not a professional degree. At least not yet. We argue that capitalism would be strengthened if managers acted as if management were a profession, whether it actually becomes one or not.

Some fear that professionalizing management means requiring businesses to be run by "professionals" and will choke the
creative energy that defines that capitalist system. To require an
MBA as a prerequisite to starting or managing a business would
foolishly limit the raw value-creating power of the brilliant entrepreneur. No one is suggesting that every business manager be
mandatorily licensed. Management is currently and foreseeably
would remain an "open" field where graduate degrees are not
required for general participation but are accorded a certain
value by various market actors or sectors. The market will drive
the desirability or necessity of the professional degree.

The history of the Hippocratic oath offers pertinent lessons for
thinking through the establishment of a professional code for
business. Many assume that the Hippocratic oath is a sacred
medical creed that has been passed on from one generation of
doctors to the next since the time of Hippocrates. In fact, until
the middle of the twentieth century, only a minority of physicians
took the oath. Interestingly, a 1928 survey by the Association of
American Medical Colleges found that only 19 percent of medical schools in North America required their students to take the
oath at graduation. It was only after World War II and the shocking discovery of gruesome experiments conducted in the name
of "medicine" that a majority of medical schools adopted the
oath in earnest. Now that the world has discovered some of the
shocking experiments conducted in the name of "financial innovation," the time is ripe for the adoption of an oath by which business practitioners conduct their activities. The human impact of
their experimentation is immeasurable, touching in some way

nearly every person on the globe. We have at this moment an unusual opportunity to try the experiment again by establishing a code for management. Now is the time for business education to re-launch the great, but delicate experiment, designed to benefit society by creating a class of business leaders who see in their work a responsibility to serve, to create value, and to lead responsibly.

3

A HIPPOCRATIC OATH
FOR BUSINESS

This is just as important as the oath doctors and lawyers take; it speaks to the "think beyond personal gain" aspect that is often absent in business today. This oath also highlights the positive role that business can play in our society.

Tim Keller, State Senator, New Mexico; Harvard, Class of 2005, signer #1675

One of Harvard University's great commencement traditions is the march of degree candidates into Harvard Yard on graduation day. The graduates gather before dawn at their respective schools, festooned in caps and gowns, and proceed slowly into the great yard. A tradition has taken hold wherein graduate students each carry symbols of their schools as they march. The law students carry gavels. The medical students wear stethoscopes. Family and friends of the graduates laugh when they see the forestry students with twigs affixed to their caps and the divinity students with golden halos made of pipe cleaners. The business students, however, traditionally prompt the biggest reaction from the gathered throng. Every year the MBAs march in waving hundred-dollar bills. And every year the crowd boos at the garish display. Every year it happens. Every year, that is, until the year we graduated. That year, students carried either flags from their home nation or a small blue card on which was printed the MBA Oath.

⸻

The MBA Oath is an affirmation of past values, a return to the founding purpose of business education to professionalize management. The oath seeks to reaffirm fundamental principles of business ethics, principles of right conduct, honesty, and value creation. This can be done within the confines of a capitalistic and democratic value system where individual initiative is rewarded at the same time as societal interests are protected.

Presently, the MBA Oath is an act of insurrection—a rebellion against the self-satisfied status quo. Over time, however, we hope that it will represent the new consensus. We intend for this to happen. The secretary of the Treasury has opined about how "capitalism will be different" from here on out. GE CEO Jeff Immelt has stated that companies have to "fundamentally reset" the way they work. Across business, people recognize that something must change. Business as usual is a recipe for disaster now not only from the standpoint of public relation perceptions but from the standpoint of real-world business practices and reality.

The MBA Oath is a response to a recent and quiet cultural change, unnoticed until now because it has happened so gradually. It is the steady movement away from a system of informal rules for conduct enforced by members of a profession toward a system of forced constraint mandated by outside regulators. As Fareed Zakaria has presciently written, "One of the great shifts taking place in American society has been away from the old guild system of self-regulation."[1] The tension between personal freedom and social duty felt by members of professions like law, medicine, and accounting has slowly been tilting away from public responsibility. More and more, the professions rely on government rather than themselves to set the rules of conduct.

Consider the law. An unfortunate shift in values has occurred among lawyers, whereby many perceive themselves less as counselors of their clients and more as zealous advocates. Elihu Root, a leading New York attorney of the late nineteenth century, captured the spirit of legal "counsel" at the time when he said, "About half the practice of a decent lawyer consists in telling would-be clients that they are damned fools and should stop."[2] The zealous advocate, on the other hand, advertises himself as nothing short of a gunslinger on behalf of a client, willing to shoot up the entire town to advance his client's interests and secure the contingency fee. The lawyer becomes less a trusted counselor and more a "bulldog determined to get *you* the biggest judgment in court."

Similarly, physicians have been challenged by the economic self-interests of their profession. Unbridled competition has led to the competitive rather than cooperative medical care in which untold fortunes are being spent on the latest technology and most advanced diagnostic equipment to entice patients to one hospital rather than another. Physicians may privately lament the social costs of such treatment but may ignore such matters in the interest of protecting their business and professional interests. The fault lines of fear and greed have driven up the costs of medicine as well as law.

"Bankers," writes Fareed Zakaria, "similarly once saw themselves as being stewards of capital, responsible to their many constituents and embodying trust. But over the past few decades, they too became obsessed with profits and the short term, uncertain about their own future and that of their company."[3] Whether you study law, medicine, accounting, banking, or virtually any other area of the private sector endeavor, you will see similar trends. Systems of self-control are breaking down. Breaches of personal and public trust have led to the demise of the self-regulating guild system, a system that was fundamental to the foundation of a well-functioning capitalistic system. The failure in self-regulation was described brilliantly by Charles Handy, a cofounder of London Business School, in a piece of required reading for all Harvard MBAs:

> Markets rely on rules and laws, but those rules and laws in turn depend on truth and trust. Conceal truth or erode trust, and the game becomes so unreliable that no one will want to play. The great virtue of capitalism—that it provides a way for the savings of society to be used for the creation of wealth—will have been eroded. So we will be left to rely increasingly on governments for the creation of our wealth, something that they have always been conspicuously bad at doing.[4]

What has occurred is the breach of public trust across a variety of professional disciplines. Community-based moral leadership has been abdicated in favor of self-interest, self-protection, and narrow ambition. As former Medtronic CEO Bill George described the situation, "The root cause of the economic crisis wasn't subprime mortgages; it was subprime leadership."

The most important thing to realize is that the MBA Oath addresses the kinds of issues business leaders typically encounter, regardless of *whether or not an oath exists.* The question is, What principles will guide your thinking when you decide? We believe the oath provides a useful framework for those decisions. We want to professionalize management by setting higher standards for MBAs. We want to promote accountability and responsibility for MBAs who take the oath and encourage the entire business community to set higher ethical standards whether they take the oath or not. We start with MBAs because that is who we are, but we believe these principles can be adopted by any leader in business.

===

Will it work?

Two questions remain. First, does our oath make sense? In other words, is it the right oath? Does it cover the right things in the right ways? That is really what the second half of the book is about—exploring each element of the oath, explaining its importance, and applying it to real-world business problems.

The second question is whether this or any oath will make a difference. Does it matter? Should we desire or expect that an oath will actually influence the world of business? We believe the oath will make a difference, for four primary reasons: meta-norming, triggering, framing, and nudging.

Meta-norming

On January 20, 2009, Barack Obama made history, taking office as the forty-fourth president of the United States. Obama and Supreme Court Chief Justice John Roberts also made history that day in another way. When the chief justice administered the oath of office to the president-elect, they fumbled the language. Few people would have noticed, except perhaps a few constitutional scholars, but later that day, Obama and Roberts met again, in the Oval Office, to readminister the oath. A nice gesture, to be sure, but was it necessary? After all, didn't they get the gist of it? Did the particular words really matter?

The fact is, words do matter. They have always mattered. Oaths are as old as human history. In the ancient Middle East, people made their vows with sobering symbolism. When someone made an oath, he would cut an animal in half and walk between the two pieces. The action symbolized the sentiment: if I break this oath, let me be like this animal. Though we have migrated to more humane means of promise making, as a society, we still believe in the power of spoken promises. The examples are numerous. To become a citizen, you must take an oath of citizenship to the United States. To testify in court, you must swear to tell the truth—all of it. To get married, you must vow to love your spouse unconditionally, whatever the circumstances. To become president, you have to take an oath of office to defend the Constitution, and you have to get the words right. As a culture, we believe in the power of public pronouncements. Practically speaking, in a courtroom, why would a jury believe the testimony of someone who refused to promise they were telling the truth? Who would marry someone who refused to remain loyal in sickness and in health? The premise of the MBA Oath lies on the principle that if we really mean to do something, we'll make a public commitment; and if we make a public commitment, we are expected to keep it.

Of course, promises, we know, are a necessary but insufficient condition for guaranteeing that the promise maker will remain a promise keeper. The divorce rate is enough to tell you that. In the business world, a company code made the difference when

James Burke dealt with the Tylenol crisis, but Enron's sixty-four-page ethics manual proved powerless in the hands of its leaders. In light of this, why would a code like the Hippocratic oath garner the respect and adherence of the entire medical profession (which is much more complicated to govern than an individual company)?

Political scientist Robert Axelrod has published several papers that show how a shared ethical orientation and set of common ideals at the *professional* level is crucial in guiding the behavior of individuals at the *company* level. He calls these ideals meta-norms, or norms that are even deeper than the culture of a particular local organization. They are enforced by punishing those who fail to punish those who break the norms. Meta-norms, Khurana and Nohria explain, "emerge partly out of an inward sense of vocation— a conviction that one is doing work that is meaningful—but are also grounded in a commitment to peer sanctions and monitoring. For example, U.S. military cadets promise 'not to lie, cheat, or steal'; they also promise 'not to tolerate those who do.' In this way, according to Axelrod, meta-norms contribute to the self-governance capability of a profession: Managers who swear to uphold a common professional code, understanding that if they violate the code they might suffer sanctions administered by their peers, are more likely to adhere to individual company codes."[5] Whereas norms function as rules within a local firm, meta-norms go beyond and address the intent and ideals of an entire class of firms. It is good to be a doctor educated at the University of California–Berkeley, but it is even more important to be a doctor because doctors as a larger group have a self-policing duty. Similarly, it is good to be a Kellogg MBA or a Stanford MBA, but it should be more important to be an MBA, period.

Interestingly, the etymological root of the word *profession* is the

Latin word *profitēri*, meaning "public declaration." Thus, a professional is distinguished from other vocations by a public declaration, a public affirmation of one's ideals and intentions. Once a public declaration is uttered, the public is invited to take notice, and a duty arises on the part of the declarant to proceed with his affairs in a manner consistent with the public declaration of his intentions.

Another way to approach the effectiveness of an oath is to consider whether the counterparty interacting with the oath taker finds value in the oath. To paraphrase Khurana, all things being equal, as a patient, I'd rather go to the surgeon who took the Hippocratic oath than the one who didn't. If I found out a doctor hadn't taken the oath, I would be concerned about whether she had my best interests in mind. What's wrong with this person? What else is motivating her?

Triggering

Dan Ariely is a behavioral scientist at MIT who has written at length about the phenomenon of cheating. He describes an experiment where students are asked to take a test. A control group was given the test and given no opportunity to cheat. A second group was given the opportunity to cheat. A third group was also given the same opportunity to cheat, but before taking the test, they were asked to read the Ten Commandments. The study found that the second group scored more highly than the control group, suggesting that they actually cheated. The third group however scored the same as the control group, suggesting that this group did not cheat. The study indicates that if people are reminded of moral values, they are more likely to act in accordance with those values.

What is remarkable is that after the test the third group could not even remember the Ten Commandments. They did not have to deeply internalize the commandments in order for the commandments to make a difference. They just had to read them. Ariely was studying a phenomenon familiar to social psychologists called "triggering." Triggering occurs when a small stimulus, or trigger, provokes a reaction. Researchers have found that people constantly act in response to triggers, even though they may not be aware of what those triggers are.

In a famous experiment, researchers administered a math test to three groups of Asian American schoolgirls. The control group was given only the math test. A second group was asked a demographic question about their gender before the test. This group performed more poorly than the control group. A third group was asked a demographic question about their ethnicity but was not asked about their gender. In the end, this group performed even better than the control group.

The three groups of girls were identical in every way. The only difference was whether they were asked about their gender or their ethnicity. And yet those differences appeared to account for the differences in their performance on the test. It was a shocking finding. The researchers were investigating whether stereotypes have any tangible effect on performance. They found that they do. When the children were reminded that they were female, it triggered in them all the cultural stereotypes of women not being as good at math as men. As a result, the stereotype became the reality and they actually did perform at a lower level. When another group of girls were reminded that they were Asian, it triggered in them all the cultural stereotypes about Asians being good at math. Again, the stereotype became the reality, and they actually performed at a higher level.

Both Ariely and the scientists who ran the math test were researching how small, seemingly trivial triggers can effect enormous change in the behavior of people. Simply reading ten lines of a moral text can make the difference between a cheater and a moral person. Simply checking a demographic box on a test can mean the difference between a child being labeled "gifted" or "below average." It does not take much. In fact, it takes so little that the person who has been triggered often does not remember the triggering event. It bears repeating that after the test, the test takers in Ariely's Ten Commandments experiment did not recall the Ten Commandments. The test takers in the math experiment could not recall which, if any, demographic questions had been asked of them. But somewhere deep inside them they "knew" and that knowledge changed the way they behaved.

By analogy, the same principles should apply to the MBA Oath. The oath could be a triggering device, just like the Ten Commandments in Dan Ariely's experiment and the demographic questions in the math test. Even without individuals knowing it, they could be affected by the oath just by having it present as a reminder. A marketing director deciding how to pitch his company's product sees his signed copy of the oath in a frame on his office wall. As he is pondering whether or not to oversell the product, seeing the oath subconsciously triggers in him a reminder of his pledge to represent the performance and risks of his company accurately. He may not even be aware of it but it will still affect him.

Framing

Of course, triggers can have an immediate impact on conduct, but what about several hours, days, or even months after the trigger has been pulled? You might wonder if the ethical impact of reading the Ten Commandments right before taking a test will have any lasting effect the next day, week, or month. The farther from the triggering event, the less impact the trigger will have. This same logic has been used as a critique of the MBA Oath. The oath may make graduates feel inspired to act professionally as they graduate, but will it continue to affect their judgment after a few months in the real world of business?

One way the oath could continue to remain a viable tool for assessing business-oriented ethical problems is to utilize the tool as a framework for making all decisions. Problems rarely present themselves in a clear, well-defined manner. On the contrary, many times it is often hard to even define the problem, to understand what the problem actually *is*. The key is recognizing problems and "framing" them correctly. In visual arts, the right frame can focus one's attention on the key part of a photograph or painting. The wrong frame can ruin it. The same is true for framing business decisions. Your best shot at getting to the right answers is asking the right questions. If you frame the problem correctly, you are asking the right questions.

For example, imagine you are the director of an oil company and you learn about an explosion at one of your oil fields. How do you think about the explosion? Is it a public relations problem to be covered up? A public safety problem to report to nearby governments? A logistics and production problem that will inhibit your ability to meet your monthly numbers? A legal liability problem? An investor confidence problem? A workplace safety problem? How you frame the situation will determine how you respond to it. Leaders need to be wary not to frame the situation too broadly or too narrowly.[6]

Let's compare two approaches to the oil explosion problem.

One approach would be to use the explosion as an occasion to rethink the fundamental strategy and to drive changes that were desirable but hard to make before. It might be an opportunity to engage the board and governmental regulatory groups to redefine the company's role with respect to employee safety.

Another plan would be to approach the situation as "damage control." This was a onetime event. It is an embarrassment or a nuisance. This frame would lead the manager to avoid exploring deeper root causes of the explosion, and instead focus on repairing the field and getting it into a productive state as quickly as possible. Either approach might be right. But the second approach is simply easier. The danger is that if the second approach is taken when the first approach is the one required, the company may suffer similar calamities in the future.

The MBA Oath will be most effective five, ten, fifteen years down the line if oath takers use the oath as a framework for decision making. This practice of framing issues with the oath could begin as soon as someone learns about the oath, but will likely only be continued if we build a long-term community of practice around the ideals of the MBA Oath.

Ideally, an oath can so subtly and fundamentally reframe one's perspective that one does not even notice it has happened. If I internalize the principles in the MBA Oath, then I will make every business decision not by looking *at* the oath, but by looking *through* it. Like a pair of glasses, the oath will focus my vision and frame my point of view. MBAs learn frameworks and practice using the frameworks in case studies to develop habits of seeing. If we start using the MBA Oath as a framework, as a habit of seeing, we will consistently see patterns in business problems that encompass ethical issues.

Nudging

Behaving ethically is more important than signing an oath, but signing an oath may be the prodding you need to actually perform ethically. Making a public statement about your intentions to behave ethically makes you more likely to keep those intentions when you need to make tough decisions. It is a way to make cognitive dissonance work for you. *Cognitive dissonance* is the uncomfortable feeling you get when you try to hold two contradictory ideas at the same time. A friend mentioned a psychological tactic that was applied to POWs in China during the Korean War to break the morale of the prisoners and cause them to betray their fellow POWs. Simply making prisoners write little statements about flaws of the United States ultimately led to greater cooperation with their captors. It is the principle of consistency; people inherently want to be consistent with their prior behavior and statements.

Richard Thaler and Cass Sunstein have written a best-selling book on the phenomenon called *Nudge*. They argue that an effective alternative to government regulating behavior is to create small incentives that "nudge" people in the right direction. They begin with the story of a woman who manages cafeterias for a large urban public school district. She found that simply by changing the locations of food on display in the cafeteria she could change the consumption patterns of students by as much as 25 percent. If she put the French fries at eye level, kids are more likely to order fries, but if she put the carrots at eye level, kids were more likely to substitute carrots for fries. Consumer products companies figured this out years ago and spend tens of millions of dollars to win prime shelf locations in grocery stores so that their cereal is placed right at eye level. They know if they can make it just a little more convenient for you, you're much more likely to choose their brand.

Analogously, giving business leaders something different to look at could change the way they lead. For years, the only things that have been at eye level are quarterly earnings and short-term profit reports. If the MBA Oath takes hold, and becomes a set of principles not just for MBAs but also for all business managers, we will be switching out the fries for the carrots. Wall Street has no shortage of reminders that it should focus on the bottom line. What it has needed is a reminder to focus on the line between right and wrong.

The oath also has an even more powerful nudge factor, one that is best explained through the metaphor of weight loss. Let's say Frank goes on a diet, but he does not tell anyone about it. He will have a hard time staying on the diet because there is no one to hold him to his goals. If the very area where Frank is weakest—self-control—is one where he does not seek help from friends, his task will be almost hopeless. On the other hand, if Frank tells his friends about the diet and describes his goal to lose weight, he will be much more likely to achieve those goals. For starters, the next time he and his friends are at the movies, Frank will be less likely to order a candy bar and double-large popcorn, for fear of the mocking or raised eyebrows it would evoke.

Many diet plans encourage dieters to either tell their family and friends that they are changing their eating habits or to join a group and get weighed regularly with others. Why? Because then you feel inherently accountable to live out the plan you said you were going to follow. It is not a guarantee of success, but those who publicly commit tend to be more successful at losing weight than those who don't.

The same dynamic is true for accomplishing any goal. Do you

want to run a marathon? Try joining a running group. Do you want to read more novels? Join a book club. Do you want to become a writer? Take a class. Stating publicly what you want to do is risky business. What happens, for example, if you fail to meet your goal? You might be embarrassed. On the other hand, if you do not tell people about your goal, you miss out on the support you could receive from them. This is true for the budding actress, the aspiring entrepreneur, and the hopeful marathoner. Any goal worth achieving is worth telling people about.

For the MBA Oath, this means telling people about your commitment to conduct yourself as a professional. By making yourself publicly accountable to your peers, you increase the likelihood of actually following through on your promises. That is why we held an oath-taking ceremony on campus at graduation. Saying the oath with your peers changes your impression of it and the significance it will have for you in the future. There is an extra accountability created by standing together with your classmates, knowing that they (and your family) see you and hear you take the oath. This serves as a powerful incentive, a strong nudge, to keep the promises.

We think signers of the MBA Oath should take up certain practices to live out the commitment they have made. For now, we are focusing on four behaviors we think will help people live the oath—writing a reflection on the oath, memorizing the oath, regularly reading about business ethics and values, and developing a few close confidantes with whom one can share questions about how to live out one's values as a professional. As our friend Elana has said, the true test of the oath is not in the moment of signing but in the thousands of small decisions that signers will make after the fact. We think that the oath itself can help in those decisions, as it creates a new meta-norm and serves as a trigger for professionalism, a frame for decision making, and a nudge toward right behavior.

In the end, we are less committed to any particular version of an oath than we are to seeing our communities and our countries strengthened by good business principles and leadership. As a movement, our goal is not to maximize the number of people who sign the oath, but to maximize the value we can create for society. Just as we believe that profit is the outcome, not the goal, of a successful business, getting people to sign our oath is not our goal, but will be the outcome if we are successful in our goal. Our goal is to encourage and support MBA graduates to be morally reflective when they make their day-to-day business decisions, to consider whether they are adding value to the whole or simply taking it for themselves.

4

SIX MORE ARGUMENTS
FOR THE MBA OATH

The MBA Oath is an outlet for me to articulate my fundamental beliefs on how a businessperson should act and lead and also a way to share and communicate my beliefs to fellow business leaders. It should be mandatory but it isn't yet. It should be enforceable but it isn't yet.

Assaf Harlap, Harvard Business School, Class of 2010,
signer #1689

In the last chapter, we laid out what we think are the four big reasons the MBA Oath could make a palpable difference in the lives of signers and in the culture of business more broadly. But we do not think that it covered all the reasons the oath is a viable idea. Also, the MBA Oath has its share of critics. While we cannot address all criticisms here because of space constraints, the following arguments for the oath will respond to many of the criticisms we hear most often. Before we get to our examination of the oath itself, we want to close part 1 of the book with six more arguments for the MBA Oath.

1. High Standards = Organizational Accountability

Google's initial public offering in 2004 was the most anticipated of the year, and perhaps the decade. In Google's articles of incorporation, the founders prominently inserted a phrase that has since become the unofficial motto of the company: "Don't be evil." In Google's early days, that phrase was a badge of honor, an example of the company's plucky courage. It was not unlike the oath of physicians: "First, do no harm." As Google grew larger, and became a more dominant force in Silicon Valley, a company with an enormous amount of power, money, and influence, critics have taken that phrase and turned it against the company. Any time that Google is accused of doing something controversial, a journalist is sure to bring up the question of whether Google is failing to abide by its own stated policy of avoiding evil.

The idea of an oath for business is not without controversy. However, one of the chief benefits of the MBA Oath is that it lays it all out there in the same way that Google's "Don't be evil" motto does. If you take the oath, you know what you are getting into and that you will be held accountable. That is a good thing, even if it is difficult. However, some people may fear creating a public standard to which they are accountable. They suggest that by subscribing to a professional code MBAs open themselves to potential liability and unnecessary investigations into their conduct. They fear that having taken the oath, their words may come back to haunt them in a courtroom or on the cover of the *Financial Times* someday. The essence of this argument is "Don't invite public scrutiny of our conduct. We don't want to be placed in a position where we may have to justify our choices to the public." They fear the risk of such scrutiny more than they fear the risk of making decisions behind closed doors, without the benefit of a searching values assessment of their choices.

To Google's credit, the motto appears to be serving a function. From the standpoint of the public and Google's critics, the motto gives them a fine hook to attach a leash. To the extent Google may ever contemplate doing something "evil," any such inclinations will no doubt be forestalled by thoughtful voices in the company reminding their colleagues of the motto and the public consequences of such a decision. Whether Google intended it or not, the public takes Google's words at face value. When a member of the public reminds Google of its famous motto, Google is required to look at its own conduct and consider whether its choice in any given circumstance is in conformance with the company's stated goals. The motto serves as an effective monitor in allowing the public a voice in commenting upon or criticizing Google's actions. In this sense, Google has boldly and courageously invited public accountability through the utterance of a simple phrase.

MBAs may be subject to potential criticism if they take the oath. If the criticism is justified, then the oath has served a purpose—by allowing the public and others to test the value of any given choice against the precepts of the oath. Such scrutiny will cause those inclined to violate its provisions to think twice before doing so. Yes, the oath may some day be waved in someone's face as he leaves his business establishment, handcuffed and in the custody of a deputy U.S. marshal. So be it. Being held publicly accountable for the value choices you make and being held accountable for violation of your words or trust is a burden necessary to the functioning of an orderly society.

Another related concern is that the MBA Oath will unfairly penalize the good guys. If not everyone is playing by the same rules of the game, it stands to reason those who play by tougher rules may find themselves at a competitive disadvantage. Thus, the argument is posed that adopting a higher moral standard may slow your ascent to the top of the corporate ladder, at least in the short-term. Analogously, viewed from the top, if a company chairman insists on a higher moral standard or company code of conduct, it will affect the way the company does business—and performance will be hurt.

The same argument has been posed in the past with respect to business dealings of nations. When Britain decided to abolish slavery, British businesses were placed at a competitive disadvantage. As long as other countries allowed slavery, British labor costs would be uncompetitively high. Was this sufficient justification for Britain to continue the slave trade? Imagine the argument from the dissenters: "We will lose our competitive advantage. The Dutch will catch up. What will we do with the colonies?" Eventually, however, through the tireless leadership of one of history's most courageous politicians, William Wilberforce, the British parliament abolished the practice of slavery simply because it was the right thing to do. In the short run, no doubt it was costly. In the long run, the costs were negligible, and the benefits were immeasurable.

Oath takers are not doe-eyed optimists who naively assume that if you do the right thing, you will always be rewarded. Wilberforce and the other British reformers faced many hostile challenges to their views, especially from constituents who lost jobs as a result of the abolition of slavery. Moral decisions can in fact be costly. On the other hand, a values-oriented choice can be the far more profitable choice in the long run. For example, what might happen in the long-term to a company that follows a moral standard? The company will conceivably enjoy the positive externalities of trust created by following the high standard. Employees will be proud of the company and more willing to make sacrifices to see it succeed. People will name the company as a preferred employer, making it easier to recruit quality staff. The company will also enjoy the trust of other firms, lowering transaction costs. Firms have an interest in developing a reputation for fairness, honesty, reliability, and generosity. Francis Fukuyama writes in his book *The Great Disruption,* that these virtues actually become economic assets and are sought even by individuals and firms interested solely in the bottom line.

2. Our Troubles Are Not All Behind Us

The cynical argue that the MBA Oath is another instance of shutting the stable door after the horse has bolted. We are struggling through the biggest financial crisis in eighty years but the damage has already been done. Are we a day late and fifty trillion dollars short? Unfortunately, the piper's bill may not yet be paid. There may be more horses in the barn.

Those who have studied economic history know the sobering truth. The crisis of 2008 is just one of dozens like it that have happened since the dawn of capitalism. Asset bubbles can grow and implode in tulip bulbs, as happened to the Dutch in 1636; in real estate, like in Japan in the late 1980s; foreign investment (Mexico in the early 1990s); or stocks in a sector (like the U.S. Internet bubble of the late 1990s). We have a bad habit of thinking that the most recent crisis will be the last one, that it hurt so bad we will not let it happen again. But a few years later asset prices start bubbling up again and we repeat the cycle. Robert Bruner recently authored a book on the panic of 1907. Commenting on the book, he said, "I witnessed a learning and a forgetting in society as the economic cycle rose and fell. We learned hard lessons from panics and crashes, but as the economy recovers, there is a tendency to assume we've corrected the cause of the most recent debacle and the future will be different."[1] Unfortunately, people's memories are short and we forget the lessons we learned.

The trouble is that investors unceasingly oscillate between two risks: the risk of losing money and the risk of missing a chance to make money. It is a struggle between greed and fear, and it usually overpowers any lessons we learn from history. When times are bad, we fear the downside risk too much and when times are good we fear it too little. During the years in between the previous financial crisis (tech stocks) and the most recent crisis (real estate and all stocks), investors mostly were concerned only with maximizing their returns. The only risk they protected against was the risk of missing out. Then, when prices started plummeting, the conversation changed. Nervous spouses began telling their partners over dinner, "We can't afford to lose any more money." The fear of missing out vanished quickly, and the fear of losing money reigned. When this crisis passes, we can only assume that the pendulum will swing again.[2]

Business will continually face these swings of the pendulum. Though spurned investors may be cautious for a time, eventually asset prices will begin to rise and we will begin hearing those familiar conversations again, about how the time to invest has never been better. A horse has bolted, but indeed the stable is filled with other horses. The time has come to manage the stable door with a new determination, a determination born of the will to elevate our interests to a higher level. It will never be too late to make that choice. Bill Pollard, the former CEO of ServiceMaster, notes, "The up and down cycles of the economy cannot be eliminated—but we can do a much better job of constraining and managing the natural forces of greed and self-interest."[3]

The MBA Oath is not simply a commitment to integrity and ethics. It is also a commitment to wise decision making that creates long-term value. A professional code of ethics is an important and worthwhile endeavor with or without a financial crisis. In good times and in bad, a code should guide our actions and decisions along the path of truth, integrity, and performance. The financial crisis was not the sole reason to launch the oath, though it was the impetus that set the reform process in motion.

The systemic risks are and will continue to be as great as or greater than the local risks facing individual firms. To illustrate: let's say a farmer in an orchard decided to tend one tree only without thought of the other trees in the orchard. For a time, that one tree might thrive by ingesting all of the nutrients and water from the orchard, and the other trees will wither. But when it comes time in the spring for that tree to receive cross-pollination from the other trees in the orchard, none will be available to pollinate that tree, and the tree will bear no fruit. That tree too will die. What business leaders must understand is that their firms thrive in community with other businesses and thrive by reason of the optimistic participation by laypersons in the marketplace. Business is organically related to the whole of the community. It cannot thrive if it undervalues and fails to appreciate the significance of its relationship with the greater community it purports to serve.

3. This Is More Than a PR Campaign

Our purpose in creating the oath is not and never has been to simply change public *perception* about MBAs. Our ultimate goal is to cause MBAs to actually *be* more responsible. In times of crisis, you either improvise and cobble together your values as you go, or you rely on the ones you have thoughtfully assented to beforehand. We think the latter is the far better option. Moreover, by fostering a broader business culture of responsibility in which certain behaviors are overtly encouraged or even presumed, we think it will be easier for a greater number of leaders to boldly do the right thing when they face difficult situations.

Not everyone believes this is our goal. One blogger felt like the oath is simply a marketing ploy for MBA programs. In an online discussion, one Wharton student responded to such critiques as follows: "Is the MBA Oath a form of marketing? Perhaps it is, but is that bad? It's a campaign that is promoting responsible management. And it's creating thoughtful discussion about important issues. Does it guarantee ethical behavior? Of course not. But it can't hurt."

We believe a professional oath for MBAs will make a difference in public perception, but more important, the oath is intended to make a difference in the lives of those who commit to its precepts. Will some fall by the wayside and forsake their words? Undoubtedly. Will some who take the oath live to regret their words some day? Probably. Will some be mocked for having made such promises and having failed to keep them? Without a doubt. This, however, is saying nothing more than what we already know about human frailty. To the extent the oath causes one to think twice before making the wrong choice, that momentary pause may make the difference between walking one path and walking another far darker path.

As we have said, the oath operates as a fault line finder. It serves to provoke examination not just of others' shortcomings and weaknesses but also one's own fault lines. If one were to paste a copy of the oath on one's dashboard and see it every day as one drives to work, it will either change the way that person does business or that person will eventually tear it from the dashboard.

The question behind the concern about whether the MBA Oath is just PR will have meaning if someone signs it and goes on to flagrantly violate it. What would happen, for instance, if Jeff Skilling, the mastermind of the Enron scandal, took the oath? Anyone can use "appearances" to deceive or mislead another. And the chance obviously exists that someone could use their signing of the oath as evidence that they are a person to be trusted, and that could lead to a manipulative deceit. Thus, bad boys will be bad boys; they can misuse the trust placed in them by appearing to be one thing and then becoming another.

On the other hand, for every Jeff Skilling, how many will be dissuaded from stepping over the line because of their public commitment to the oath? In other words, even though one horse is out of the barn, how many will stay in place—even with the door wide open? One can only wonder what might have happened if Jeff Skilling had signed the oath and had been committed to a partnering relationship with a fellow oath signer for the duration of his career.

Who in fact signs the oath? Broadly speaking, one can assume three groups may sign the oath—all for different reasons. Let us call them the Angels, the Weasels, and the Fence-sitters. The Angels are people who plan to follow the precepts of the oath regardless of whether they take the oath or not. For them, signing the oath may be nothing more than a public affirmation of their principles. In business school parlance, they are "low-hanging fruit" for the MBA Oath movement. However, even the Angels may intend their signing of the oath to serve as an inducement to others to sign. For them, this is an opportunity to build up the reservoir of trust among business managers and to more readily identify those with whom they wish to partner in business in the future.

The Weasels are people who have no intention of making good on the oath but sign because they want to be perceived as ethical. For them the oath may be a mere formality at best or at worst a manipulative tool to build the unwitting trust of a potential business victim. The third group, the Fence-sitters (those who are on the fence) are the most important because they are the ones for whom the oath may serve the greatest benefit.

The Fence-sitters are probably the largest group. Weasels and Angels are harder to find, and most people simply glide along either unwilling to make a choice or at least disinterested in choosing unless their hand is forced. What will prompt them to choose? When they do choose, what will influence them? A public declaration is more likely to cause a correct choice than no declaration at all.

In reality, no one is either all good or all bad or even all undecided. Some Angels will fall and some Weasels will eventually be redeemed. To the extent the oath reduces the casualties among the Angels and restores the Weasels to full ethical health, the prescription and the medicine offered by the oath is designed to prevent the casualty list from growing exponentially. The oath is not just a snapshot, capturing the ethical commitments one makes at a specific point in time. It also serves to continually prompt and prod good choices. The bottom line is that we wish Jeff Skilling had signed the oath. If history were to be rewritten, we would rather risk the future with a Jeff Skilling who signed the oath than the Jeff Skilling who did not.

Finally, we recognize and acknowledge that the oath can be reduced to "check-the-box" integrity. We are even aware of one business school admissions consulting Web site that has counseled prospective business school applicants to make sure they align themselves with the pledges if they want to be admitted. We would encourage admissions counselors to advise prospective applicants of the importance of the oath and caution them that business schools are increasingly going to be considering applications measured against the standards of the oath. In that regard, admissions departments should not be satisfied with a simple check-box response to such inquiries but should require real-life anecdotal accounts of how prospective students have applied analogous standards in their own lives. We encourage business school admissions departments to seriously consider scrutinizing applications from the standpoint of the precepts of the oath.

4. Character Alone Is Not Enough

Some will argue that though they believe people should behave ethically, they contend that the oath is unnecessary because inner character, not uttered promises, will eventually guide good business conduct. This view fails to appreciate that in business words alone signify character. In other words, when one says his word is his bond, it means the words he speaks carry power and conviction. Thus, character is revealed in the words. The words themselves are the conduct portraying the character.

Character, in and of itself, however, is not always reliable, particularly in the heat of the battle. As the premise of this book suggests, we all have fault lines, and no one has a perfect character. These fault lines in character are many times invisible to those whose character is in issue. Significant data have been marshaled by social psychologists indicating that one's "context" may be a more powerful governor of behavior than character. We will discuss this in chapter 6 when we review the experiments of Yale psychologist Stanley Milgram and others. The oath is intended to be a standard by which character may be judged and confirmed. The oath suggests that one's commitment to certain behaviors will reveal whether one has the requisite character and appreciation of ethical norms and values to lead a values-oriented business.

We agree that MBAs do not need an oath to be ethical. Indeed, a witness does not need to swear to tell the truth in court in order to actually tell the truth. A groom does not need to swear to care for a woman in sickness and in health in order to actually do so in marriage. The promise is not an enabling mechanism that unlocks powers previously inaccessible to the promise maker. The promise is instead a tool of accountability. In the heat of battle, character is often compromised. Those are precisely the moments when the oath may best serve the interests of business and the public. The oath assists you and others in defining the line between what is acceptable and what is not. When the chips are down, pressure is turned up and time is short; the temptation is to do what seems best in terms of one's narrow self-interest in the short run. In these situations, the impetus to turn away from short-term selfish advantage to long-term sustainable value is embodied in the principles of the oath. The oath places those values on the table, directly in front of your nose. Will you forsake those values or will you uphold them?

We acknowledge that many of those who subscribe to the MBA Oath are likely to be people who would abide by its principles regardless of whether they took the oath or not. The oath standing alone may not be the reason they participate in or abstain from unethical or unwise business choices. That does not mean that even the most conscientious and moral person is free of moments of moral or ethical ambiguity. The oath serves to remind and anchor as much as it serves to prod and motivate.

The MBA Oath initiative is grounded in the wisdom of the group as a whole. One person did not write the MBA Oath. From the beginning, it was an entirely cooperative and group-oriented initiative. The strength of the movement arises from the fact that it is premised on consensus-building, not isolated and independent acts of individuals. We seek to develop a critical mass, a "tipping point," where the cultural norms are transformed, standards of conduct are raised and become exceedingly difficult to subvert.

For the foregoing reasons, we encourage MBA students to not sign the oath alone but to seek out at least a few other signers from their school to take the oath. In this way, they will create an accountability network of peers. Additionally, we are building a network of "chapters" on the campuses of the world's top business schools. One of the requirements of becoming an official chapter is getting at least 30 percent of the graduating class each year to sign the oath. We want to create sizable populations of students at each of these schools so that the students will feel like they have the support they need to live out the oath after they graduate.

5. We Cannot Rely on the Law Alone

"Why should business regulate itself?" we have heard some MBAs ask. Business is what business does. If someone does not like the way business is conducted, let the politicians pass a law. If the law is silent, why not take advantage of the circumstance? As long as the legal line is not crossed, who can complain? The law will take care of the really bad fellows. If that's not good enough, let them try to pass more laws.

This argument confuses law and responsibility. The presupposition is that by merely following the law one satisfies society's requirements and expectations of morality in business dealings and judgment. Whether the law and morality are synchronous at any given moment is a matter of debate. Many lawyers will tell you to save arguments about morality and the law for a "higher realm" because the law is premised on expedience and necessity, not morality.

Besides, most people expect more of business than the law demands. The Millennium Poll, which interviewed over twenty-five thousand citizens across twenty-three countries on six continents in May 1999, found that two in three people want companies to go beyond their historical role of making a profit, paying taxes, employing people, and obeying all laws: "They want companies to set a higher ethical standard and contribute to broader societal goals as well."[4] If people are suspicious of capitalism, it is because they believe that corporations have no purpose other than serving themselves.

As we will discuss later, the business equivalent of medicine's "Do no harm" means that we are committed, if necessary, to going beyond mere legal responses. The law's requirements are standards for practice, but true business professionals should not categorize ethics in terms of the minimal standards of the law. Of course, we should create laws that are useful and regulations that restrain unfettered greed, but we must recognize that generally the law usually lags behind best practice. We can do better.

Consider this: in response to the financial crisis, legislators are enacting new laws and regulations. From setting leverage limits to limiting executive compensation to regulating securities trading, the government is becoming a more active participant in the financial system than it has been in decades. The government is now becoming a primary stakeholder in many private business endeavors. We are seeing increased government regulation and government "partnership" or "ownership" interests in private business. If you run a business, the specter of increased government oversight is not always welcome. However, increased regulation is the result of businesses failing to regulate themselves. Stepped-up regulation increases transaction costs, requires more tax dollars to support oversight, and hampers business competitiveness.

Aleksandr Solzhenitsyn, winner of the Nobel Prize in Literature, spoke at Harvard's commencement in 1978 to remind students of the consequences for a society without a moral compass. After World War II, he was arrested for criticizing the Soviet government and sentenced to work for years in the Gulag. Solzhenitsyn's address was sobering, because he noted that he was increasingly finding in the West a growing dependence upon law alone to guide behavior. "A society with no other scale but the legal one is not quite worthy of man . . . [it] is taking very scarce advantage of the high level of human possibilities. The letter of the law is too cold and formal to have a beneficial influence on society. Whenever the tissue of life is woven of legalistic relations, there is an atmosphere of moral mediocrity, paralyzing man's noblest impulses."[5] Relying on the law creates a culture of negative limits that we press and long to exceed. What we need is a culture of positive aspirations that we press and long to meet. Is it better to just do what you need to do so you don't create injustice? Or is it better to work for justice? The difference is clear.

6. This Is a Good First Step

Despite our expressed high ideals, will the culture of business eat us for breakfast? As a writer for *Newsweek* commented, after graduation, MBAs do not take their training into a vacuum—we join an ecosystem with its own regulations and incentives, and these can prove more significant than classroom lessons, or graduation pledges.

The blunt truth is if the system is the problem, then the system must be changed. How does one change an entire system? By rewriting the rules. Unless the fundamental orienting values of the system are changed, the system will squash efforts to reform it on the margins. In this regard, to paraphrase Margaret Mead, never underestimate the power of a small group of dedicated, passionate advocates to change the course of history, in business or any other field.

Major players are already stepping up to the challenge of the oath. Organizations like the Aspen Institute, the World Economic Forum, and the G-20 are exploring ways to support the idea of a new business standard like the MBA Oath. Each year, the World Economic Forum identifies two hundred to three hundred individuals drawn from around the globe to be a part of its Forum for Young Global Leaders (YGL). These leaders—from business, academia, and government—embody the multistakeholder ethos of organizational management and are already shaping the world around them. The YGL community has adopted the idea of a global business oath, and there are exciting implications for the MBA Oath. When organizations like these and their leaders, including some of the most influential business executives in the world, join the effort, the notion that the fundamental rules of the game are in the process of being rewritten is not so naive.

We acknowledge that the oath will not magically heal the problems that confront business today. There are no silver bullets. We contend, however, that the oath is not only an important first step but also an essential one. When a doctor gives a patient the aftercare instructions at the hospital, the patient cannot believe that by simply acknowledging the instructions healing will magically occur. On the contrary, the hard work begins when the patients are on their own and required to do daily exercises and take appropriate medications and take daily note of their condition. The oath itself is merely the plan of treatment. The hard work of healing will indeed begin when the oath takers face difficult decisions and are required to strain the unused and weakened muscles that must be built up in order to stand tall and walk a straight line.

How do we make the oath more than a onetime pledge, soon to be forgotten? Where are the professional teeth? Lawyers can be disbarred, doctors can lose their licenses to practice, but our oath has no such enforcement mechanism. This is a thorny issue. An honor code without an enforcement mechanism is of less value.

At present the MBA Oath has two enforcement mechanisms. The first is the implied and informal social norm enforcement arising from the fact that whoever takes the oath has their name publicly listed on our Web site, www.mbaoath.org. Coworkers, customers, clients, suppliers, and neighbors all have the ability to see whether the business manager with whom they work has or has not taken the oath. If one's name does not appear, savvy customers or clients may ask them why they have not taken the oath. If one has taken the oath, customers and clients may likewise challenge the oath taker in any given circumstance to live up to the standards described by the oath or explain the reason for any variance thereto. Because all oath takers are aware of the existence of this public list, they will have great incentive to align their actual behavior with the oath they have taken.

A second enforcement mechanism arises from our having reserved the right to remove any person from the list of oath takers for gross violation of the principles of the oath. We believe that anyone who witnesses what they believe to be an infraction against the oath should have the right to bring that accusation before our board for review. Due process will be accorded to the alleged offender to explain or justify the challenge, but if the board concludes that the signer in question has violated the oath, the potential exists that the person's name could be removed from the list. Only time will tell whether the threat of removal from the list will serve as an incentive for ethical or wise decision making.

Other possibilities include developing a professional association for MBAs that requires members to adhere to the oath as a prerequisite. The prestige of the association would serve as a further incentive to the oath takers to abide by their principles. Another interesting possibility has been proposed by an enterprising group of MBAs who have suggested we "securitize" the oath. After all, one thing we learn in business school is that you value what you pay for. We could have individual signers pay twenty-five dollars a year to maintain their status as signers. We could then utilize the funds to support local chapters hosting events to discuss the professional responsibilities of managers and the ethical dilemmas of business.

Finally, and perhaps most important, consideration must be given to encouraging business schools to adopt a policy wherein taking the oath or some variation thereof is a necessary prerequisite to earning a degree. In 2010, respected media outlets such as the *Economist* and the *Financial Times* are calling for change in business school curriculums and pointing to the MBA Oath as a good start. Perhaps officially adopting the MBA Oath is where schools could begin their reforms.

In the final analysis, the nature of any enforcement mechanism is going to be entirely dependent upon the organic growth of the MBA Oath movement in the university community, the business community, and the public-at-large community. As we previously mentioned, the MBA Oath is a working document, not yet hammered in stone. Over time, we expect the oath will be edited and amended by future generations of MBAs. We are open to amendment and refinement of the oath's statements.

What is important is to comprehend and engage the oath at the level of principle. Many are anxious to begin speculation as to the application of the oath in particular circumstances. Critics argue that the oath needs to be more specific, taking a position on more granular issues rather than just setting forth abstract principles. This argument fails to take account of the myriad circumstances of business and life in which laying down a hard-line boundary may solve one problem but create another. When physicians take their oath, they do not promise to use aspirin in every instance to fight a fever. Lawyers do not take an oath to advise every tax client to maximize certain deductions. Hard-line issue-oriented provisions in the oath are not realistic and will likely date the oath in the long run.

What is necessary is a body of long-standing principles, an overarching structure upon which the remainder of the building may be fashioned as time and circumstance demand. We now shift our attention to those principles, to understand both why we included what we did and the potential that each tenet has to redefine business as usual. Throughout we draw on cases we studied during our MBA program, applying the principles of the oath to the situations we studied in class. It is time to consider what the oath actually says.

THE PRINCIPLES

THE PURPOSE OF A MANAGER

As a manager, my purpose is to serve the greater good by
bringing together people and resources to create value that
no single individual can build alone. Therefore, I will seek
a course that enhances the value my enterprise can create
for society over the long-term.

Preamble to the MBA Oath

I believe that this oath will lay the foundation for a new
generation of ethical business professionals.

Marisa Buzzanca, NYU Stern School of Business, Class of 2009,
signer #1388

You can go a long way if you are willing to ask simple questions, especially the kind that you are afraid might make
you look stupid because they are so simple. Having the
courage to ask these kinds of questions forces people to articulate
their assumptions, and those assumptions are revealing. Thus,
we would like to begin this chapter with a simple question:

What is a business for?

Take a moment and fill in the blank, "The purpose of business is _____." We have asked this question of
many intelligent people, and a lot of them are quick to give the

same answer: "The purpose of business is to maximize profits." A simple answer for a simple question. So we ask another simple question: *How does a business make a profit?* "It's simple," our friends reply. "By creating goods or services that people find valuable enough to buy for a price greater than the cost of producing them." That leads to a third question, perhaps the simplest of all: *Why would you want to make a profit?* Why make a profit? Isn't it obvious? "You make a profit so that you can increase your wealth and buy goods and services." Now things are getting interesting, because we have come full circle. The purpose of creating valuable goods and services is to obtain a profit, but the purpose of obtaining profit is to then obtain valuable goods and services. It's a circle. If we care enough to create a good product (in the form of goods and services) in order to obtain a good product, then we might logically conclude that creating our product is in itself a goal. This logic prompts us to reexamine the answer to our first question. Making a profit is often lauded as the only goal of business. Yet this answer doesn't take into account the worth of consuming a valuable product, as well as the great satisfaction of creating the valuable product.

As human beings, we are endowed with creative energies; joy and satisfaction are gained from the act of creation in itself. Not many employees wake up in the morning to create shareholder value. Similarly, few CEOs motivate employees by asking them to focus on the higher calling of maximizing profits for shareholders. None that we heard from during our two years at business school. Most CEOs strode confidently in front of the classroom and talked about creating value for customers and working with teams of employees to do great things for society. Profit is a necessary but insufficient justification for business. Just as important, a firm must create *value*. Therefore we begin the

MBA Oath with a sensible, though still controversial, premise that the purpose of management is to bring together people and resources to create long-term societal value that no individual could build alone. This value includes profit, to be sure, but our goal is not to maximize profits. It should be to maximize *value* over the long-term. Let's look at an example to see what we mean by this.

Toothpaste and Tire Repairs

Suppose two companies sell toothpaste. Big Profit Paste sells toothpaste to customers in order to make the best profit. Lasting Smiles brand earns profits as a way to manufacture the best toothpaste for its customers. For the sake of argument, let us make them extremist companies. Big Profit Paste *only* cares about making the biggest profit; Lasting Smiles *only* wants to create the most valuable toothpaste possible. Assuming all other things about these companies are the same, we might expect them to make the same decisions the vast majority of the time, and in a small minority of circumstances their different philosophies will cause their strategies to diverge.

Suppose both companies have the opportunity to substitute an ingredient with a cheaper one that lowers the cost of the product but in the long run interferes with the product's ability to fight plaque. No one will notice the new additive in the short run. The taste, look, and feel of the toothpaste remains the same. In this situation, we would expect Big Profit Paste to use the substitute ingredient because it will lower their costs and increase their profits, consistent with the company's governing values. We would expect Lasting Smiles to reject the substitute, because using the substitute would violate its goal of creating the best toothpaste possible for its customers.

Because the toothpaste looks and performs the same in the short-term, Big Profit Paste can charge the same price as Lasting Smiles and the market will not immediately punish Big Profit Paste for cutting corners. Instead Big Profit Paste m.e rewarded in the short-term. It will enjoy higher earnings, enabling it to spend more money on advertising, innovation, and distribution, giving it a competitive edge over Lasting Smiles. Given all of this, we would expect Big Profit Paste's stock price to outperform that of Lasting Smiles over a certain time horizon. Lasting Smiles may be required to endure relative underperformance while waiting for consumer knowledge and confidence to bolster a quality-driven product.

However, since Big Profit Paste's toothpaste is inferior to Lasting Smiles's, dentists or consumers will eventually figure it out. The invisible hand of the market will move, and Lasting Smiles will be able to charge higher prices or take Big Profit Paste's market share.

Which company made the better decision? We think Lasting Smiles, because it is creating an organization that is built to last. Big Profit Paste, by using inferior products in the short-term, increases its risk for consumer defection, lawsuits, and negative headlines, which could result in irreparable damage to its brand. To be clear, Big Profit Paste was not incorrect in seeking a low-cost position to outperform a competitor. This competitive maneuvering is to be admired if done in a sustainable fashion. The issue is that Big Profit Paste cut corners in a way that was to the long-term detriment of all stakeholders—customers, employees, and shareholders. Meanwhile, we would expect Lasting Smiles to capture market share and beyond once the inferior ingredients are brought to light. We would add that we would rather work for Lasting Smiles, with its uncompromising focus on high quality and sustainability. We imagine many other MBAs feel the same, and in the race for talent, we think this matters.

Tom Chappell, the founder of toothpaste maker Tom's of Maine, puts it simply: "The point of business is not to *trick* customers into buying your product, to manipulate them to your side rather than a competitor's. The goal of business should be to create a good product that will do well by the customers. The challenge of selling is to convince customers that your vision of the good coincides with their vision of the good."[1] When those two visions align, the world is literally a better place. That is when value has been created. That is when business fulfills its purpose.

In aligning their visions for the good, many times consumers rely on businesspeople to give expert and objective advice, like that which a doctor might give. Ethicist Peter Singer makes the comparison between eye surgeons and car salesmen: "A member of my family recently had an eye problem, and was referred by her general practitioner to an eye surgeon. The surgeon examined the eye, said that it didn't need surgery, and sent her back to the general practitioner. That is no more than one would expect from a doctor who is true to the ethics of the profession, my medical friends tell me. By contrast, it's hard to imagine going to a car dealer and being advised that you don't really need a new car."[2] It may be hard to imagine this happening at an auto dealer, but occasionally it does happen in business. We appreciate it when a waiter tells us which bottle of wine is the best value instead of just pushing the most expensive bottle. We are grateful when a real estate broker admits that the apartment building we are interested in has had a rodent problem. One of us recently had a tire leak and took the car to a tire service center. The mechanic at the garage looked at the tire for a few minutes and we were expecting bad news. Instead, he simply placed a patch on the old tire instead of insisting on the purchase of a new expensive tire. Was that the short-term profit-maximizing action for the tire center? No, but the action won our loyalty for the long-term.

Drilling Deeper: The Purpose of Business

In business school, we found a lot of disagreement about the purpose of business. Our classmates were divided on the subject. So were our professors. Some of the world's most successful business leaders and distinguished academics disagree about it too. For instance, consider the difference between the business philosophy of Johnson & Johnson and that of Milton Friedman.

Earlier in this book we described how James Burke led Johnson & Johnson through the Tylenol crisis by relying on the company's credo. For decades, the credo has been the centerpiece of the Johnson & Johnson culture and has, more or less effectively, guided the firm's strategy and decision making. Here is a selection of the credo:

> We believe our first responsibility is to the doctors, nurses, and patients, to mothers and fathers and all others who use our products and services. In meeting their needs everything we do must be of high quality. We must constantly strive to reduce our costs in order to maintain reasonable prices . . . Our suppliers and distributors must have an opportunity to make a fair profit. We are responsible to our employees, the men and women who work with us throughout the world. Everyone must be considered as an individual. We must

respect their dignity and recognize their merit. . . . We are responsible to the communities in which we live and work and to the world community as well . . . Our final responsibility is to our stockholders. Business must make a sound profit . . . When we operate according to these principles, the stockholders should realize a fair return.[3]

The Johnson & Johnson credo subscribes to the concept that it must first and foremost serve the needs of its customers—doctors and patients, mothers and fathers. In the process, it aims to take care of its employees, act as a good corporate citizen, and make a "sound" and "fair" profit. In other words, it highlights the company's belief that it has multiple responsibilities to fulfill. This may sound laudable to you, but some might disagree.

Milton Friedman was a Nobel Prize winner in economics at the University of Chicago. To say that his work influenced a generation of economists is an understatement. In 1970, Friedman wrote an enormously popular essay entitled, "The Social Responsibility of Business Is to Increase Its Profits." Friedman opines,

The view has been gaining widespread acceptance that corporate officials and labor leaders have a "social responsibility" that goes beyond serving the interest of their stockholders or their members. This view shows a fundamental misconception of the character and nature of a free economy. In such an economy, there is one and only one social responsibility of business—to use its resources and engage in activities designed to increase its profits so long as it stays within the rules of the game, which is to say, engages in open and free competition, without deception or fraud . . . Few trends could so thoroughly undermine the very foundations of our free society as the acceptance by corporate

officials of a social responsibility other than to make as
much money for their stockholders as possible.[4]

Friedman's thesis that "the business of business is business"
(and nothing more) is compellingly simple. Businesses have
only one goal—maximizing profits. Any other business agenda
is paternalistic, inefficient, and misguided. If the managers of a
company wants to give money away, they should give away their
own personal assets, not those of a firm they do not own.

NYU's business law professor William T. Allen creates a distinction between Johnson & Johnson's view of business and Friedman's. He identifies Friedman's perspective as the "property" view
of business. The "property" view is so-named because the corporation is seen as the *private property of its stockholder-owners*. The history of the property view is rooted in a 1919 Michigan Supreme
Court case, *Dodge v. Ford Motor Co.*[5] The Dodge brothers, shareholders of Ford Motor Company, complained that Henry Ford,
who controlled the board of directors, acted irresponsibly toward
Ford shareholders. Ford had decided that his company should
suspend further dividend payments indefinitely. He wanted the
company to retain $58 million in profits in order expand its busi-
ness and lower its prices. Henry Ford was quoted in the press as
saying that the purpose of the corporation was to produce good
products cheaply and to provide increasing employment at good
wages, and only incidentally to make money.[6] The Dodge brothers asserted that the shareholders owned the enterprise and that
they were entitled to force the directors to pay out accumulated
profits. The Michigan Supreme Court agreed, and ordered Ford
to pay the dividends.

The "property view" argues that if shareholders "own" the
corporation, then it is improper for managers to engage in any

activities that do not maximize profits. Why should executives be allowed to use other people's money to pursue their own, perhaps eccentric, views of "the public good"? Moreover, say those who hold the property view, action consistent with the property model is likely to maximize wealth creation And wealth creation in itself has a broad and positive public impact. Overall standards of living rise as wealth is created. In this way, the property view is compatible with the MBA Oath, which advocates enhancement of the value of the enterprise for the long-term benefit of the greater society. Moreover, even Friedman states that one has a responsibility to conform "to the basic rules of society, both those embodied in law and those embodied in ethical custom."[7] In other words, Friedman argues that profit maximization is restrained by cultural norms and ethical standards. Philosopher Michael Novak argues that Friedman's own definition of the purpose of business includes "a fairly extensive range of moral responsibilities, such as maintaining open and free competition, establishing a framework for the rule of law, avoiding deception and fraud, and exemplifying fair play within the rules of the game. This is altogether no small moral agenda."[8] Still, make no mistake, the property view of business states that the only consequential concern of a manager is to maximize profits for the business.

In contrast to the property view, William Allen defines the social entity view of business, which more or less aligns with Johnson & Johnson's credo. In this paradigm, investors must be assured an attractive rate of return on their investment in order to make their capital investment. However, the firm has other goals of equal or higher dignity. Under the social entity view, managers have additional obligations: to please their customers, provide meaningful work for employees, and contribute to the public good of their communities.

The social entity view of business is rooted in the fact that corporations are authorized by the state as legal *entities*. They are not purely private property. In the words of Supreme Court justice Benjamin Cardozo, they are "tinged with a public purpose." The state authorizes the creation of corporations and limits the liability of its directors and executives because it believes corporations promote the general welfare. This makes intuitive sense. If businesses did not promote the general welfare and the greater good, why would governments allow them?

A society may authorize business to create new wealth and what Adam Smith called "universal opulence," a condition he defined in which real wages of workers grow "until the once-poor live at a level that even kings and dukes did not once enjoy." A society may also authorize corporations because it wants to create jobs. When large numbers of people are unemployed, envy, resentment, and even violence grow. A few years ago, the suburbs of Paris nearly became a war zone, filled with rioters and burning cars, as unemployed young immigrants protested the lack of jobs. The point is that we need businesses, and not just because they make profits. When businesses create jobs, spread technology, improve efficiency, and increase value, they are making the world a better place to live. They are agents of progress and change.

Computer pioneer Dave Packard, one of the founders of Hewlett-Packard, sums up the entity view this way. "Many people assume, wrongly, that a company exists simply to make money. While this is an important result of a company's existence, we have to go deeper and find the real reasons for our being. People get together and exist as a company so that they are able to *accomplish something collectively that they could not accomplish separately*— they make a contribution to society, a phrase which sounds trite but is fundamental."[9] What Packard describes is the same point we make in the preamble to the oath—that the mission of a manager is to bring together people and resources to create value that no individual can create alone. A good manager will earn great profits for his company as a *result* of his work, but earning great profits is not in itself his work.

Given the distinction between the property and social entity views, which provides the better definition of the purpose of business? Should businesses exist solely to maximize shareholder returns, or do they have other purposes of equal or greater importance? While we have great respect for the logic and simplicity of the property view of business, we think the social entity concept provides a more compelling purpose for business because it recognizes three realities: that shareholders differ in their goals, that great businesses are built by creating *value*, and that focusing exclusively on profit maximization adds dangerous risk to the firm and to society.

First, shareholders differ in their goals. The truth is that in most modern corporations, the shareholders, employees, and customers are in some sense indistinguishable. Take the food company General Mills: employees are customers of the company's cereal and granola bars, and are also shareholders through stock-option grants. Given this reality, simply applying the rule of shareholder return maximization does not help a manager make decisions. If a manager employs layoffs to simply maximize the interests of his shareholders, she is simultaneously injuring the same persons in their employee capacity. Not all shareholders are alike in their profile and investment objective. A shareholder can be any of the following: an employee of the company intent on keeping his job and salary; a day trader who will own the stock for a few hours; a founder who views the company as his baby; an activist hedge fund that wants to change management; or a large public employee pension fund using its investment in the company as a nonvolatile portion of its greater portfolio. When considering bondholders, the picture gets even more cloudy. The differences between these claimants on the business are striking so managing by maximizing shareholder value alone does not provide the manager with as much clear direction as one might assume.

Second, great businesses have great vision. We have discussed why businesses exist, but not what makes them great. This answer to this question is what every manager wants to know. There is no formula, but there is a pattern. Think of a company, any company, that you believe is great and answer the question, "What makes this company great?" Maybe it is because they have superior customer service, or maybe their business strategy is unassailable, or maybe they have a knack for designing better products than those of their competitors. We doubt your answer was "because the company is so profitable." Great companies are not great simply because they are profitable. Whether it is Procter & Gamble, Walmart, Intel, General Electric, or ESPN, these companies have been financially successful because they all have done the same thing: they have created more *value* than their competitors have. Donald Soderquist, the former COO of Walmart, explains that the behemoth retailer did not become gigantic because it wanted to be gigantic; it did so in the process of pursuing another goal. "Our vision was not to become the largest company in the world, or to make the most money," he says. "Our vision was to provide a shopping environment that no one else had provided before, and to attract a group of employees who could be considered family, who were loyal and dedicated and who shared the same vision."[10]

This is not to say that profits are not important. Indeed, they are extraordinarily important. Business leaders should make profit growth one of their top priorities. However, as Charles Handy stated, "To turn shareholders' needs into a purpose is to be guilty of a logical confusion, to mistake a necessary condition for a sufficient one. We need to eat to live; food is a necessary condition of life. But if we lived mainly to eat, making food a sufficient or sole purpose of life, we would become gross. The purpose of a business, in other words, is not to make a profit, full stop. It is to make a profit so that the business can do something more or better. That 'something' becomes the real justification for the business."[11] When maximizing profits becomes the *only* goal, managers' decisions can be counterproductive for clients, society, and for the firm long-term. Investor Howard Marks gives three examples from the financial world, "A money manager's desire to add to assets under management, and thus profits, can lead him to take in all the money he can. But when asset prices and risks are high and prospective returns are low, this clearly isn't good for his clients. Selling financial products to anyone who'll buy them, as opposed to those for whom they're right, can put investors at unnecessary risk. And cajoling rating agencies into assigning the highest rating to debt backed by questionable collateral can put whole economies in jeopardy, as we've seen."[12]

Ultimately, the role of a manager is to integrate the entity and property conceptions of business. "A professional ideology of service to the greater good is not at odds with the principle of shareholder value creation," says Thunderbird School dean Angel Cabrera. "It actually grounds shareholder value morally and it integrates it in a richer multidisciplinary context. It reaffirms the importance of shareholder value as both a source of societal prosperity in itself as well as an indicator of other forms of value. But it acknowledges that businesses create multiple forms of value and it attributes to managers responsibilities that go beyond profit maximization."[13] In the end, you cannot really make a great profit without taking care of your customers and employees and creating value. Nor can you do those things without making a profit. You need to do both. In other words, let's build great businesses. Let's make profit, lots of it, not because profit is our only goal but because if we are profitable, it is an indicator that we have created value.

It is time to reassert that the purpose of business is to create societal value that no individual could create alone. What is a business for? It is for uniting private interests to bring about the public good. It is for creating more value than you extract. It is about building value for the long-term.

6

ETHICS AND INTEGRITY

I will act with utmost integrity and pursue my work in an ethical manner. My personal behavior will be an example of integrity, consistent with the values I publicly espouse.

MBA Oath, First Promise

Somebody once said that in looking for people to hire, you look for three qualities: integrity, intelligence, and energy. And if they don't have the first, the other two will kill you.

—Warren Buffett

The MBA Oath is a public statement that holds each of the members accountable to conduct business with the highest of standards on a daily basis. It is also a reminder to us all to represent ourselves to the highest level of integrity.

John Mathern, Arizona State University,
Class of 2008, signer #1706

According to the most recent data we could find, about 12 percent of soft drinks sales come from vending machines. It is a big business. In the United States alone, more than 1.2 *billion* cases of soft drinks are sold through vending machines every year. Not only is it a big business, it is a

stable one too. Nothing fancy. You load up the box with a bunch
of drinks. Thirsty consumers insert change to buy a bottle. They
slake their dry throats with your sugary beverage, and you come
back in a week to collect the money. Repeat.

Several years ago, Coca-Cola decided to spice up the bottom
line of their vending business with a technological innovation.
They rigged standard soda pop machines with a thermometer
that could detect whether it was a hot or cold day and could
then change prices depending on the weather. The idea was that
when the temperature rose, the demand for a soda increased,
so the price of the beverage in the machine would correspond-
ingly increase. This might appear to be eminently reasonable
and fair to free-market proponents, many of whom, we might
add, are MBAs. After all, there is no inherently just or fair price
for a bottle of soda, so simply charge the price that customers are
willing to pay.

The average Coke drinker, on the other hand, thought the
plan was all but treasonous. It seemed to insert a degree of arbi-
trariness and capriciousness into the sales transaction, which was
dependent upon whims of weather. It hit consumers right when
they were warmest and weakest. The public outcry was loud. The
San Francisco Chronicle called it "a cynical ploy to exploit the thirst
of faithful customers." The *Miami Herald* called Coca-Cola "soda
jerks." A seemingly simple issue on the price of a soda had ele-
vated into an ethical issue on what was fair.

Amid the controversy, Coca-Cola quickly and quietly replaced
all the new machines and returned to standard pricing. The
beverage company learned an important lesson: people have
surprisingly deep-seated feelings about what a fair price is for a
can of carbonated water and syrup. It also learned that what the

company thought was fair was a far cry from what its customers thought was fair.

The first pledge of the MBA Oath is to "act with utmost integrity and pursue my work in an ethical manner." Far from being a motherhood and apple pie statement, this may be the most difficult to fulfill of the eight MBA Oath pledges. First, what is ethical in any given situation is rarely black and white—just ask executives at Coca-Cola. Second, we are constantly faced with opportunities that tempt us to violate our own ethical values. Third, despite what we would like to believe, we are less ethical than we think. We will explore each of these difficulties in this chapter.

Despite the difficulties, the first responsibility for men and women in business is to lead ethically and with integrity. Whether in business, politics, sports, or entertainment, our culture is littered with examples of individual superstars whose failures of character either got in their way or brought them down completely. Warren Bennis, professor and author of more than twenty books on leadership, agrees: "I have never seen anyone derailed from top leadership because of a lack of business literacy or technical competence or conceptual skills. It's *always* because of lapses of judgment and questions about character."[1] Sometimes those failures do not just bring down individuals, but entire companies. And it is not hard to see how. Harvard professor Scott Snook conducted research that found that a third of MBAs define right and wrong by what is the norm as opposed to a more universal constant. The trouble is obvious: What happens when you are in a situation where the norm is to hide corporate losses or to sexually harass coworkers? If going with the "norm" is not enough, what is the alternative? What does it mean to be ethical?

The Man, the Mine Shaft, and the Meaning of Ethics

A popular story used at colleges to teach students about the diffi-culty of ethical decisions is "The Man and the Mine Shaft." Imagine you are traveling with a group of twenty hikers through a remote forest. You discover an abandoned mine shaft, and in a moment of bad judgment you decide to go in and explore. Your team lights torches and makes it about fifty meters in when, without warning, you hear a rumble, then a roar of rock on rock. You turn to see the landslide and watch hopelessly as the entrance to the mine col-lapses. The entire team is panicked. You do not know what to do. You are not ready for this. As the dust settles you see a shaft of light coming through the now blocked entrance. Miraculously, there is a narrow crawl space. Then you notice one of the members of your group, a large man, running to the opening. You try to stop him, but before you can do anything, he has himself halfway through the crawl space and then . . . he gets stuck. Not only does he get stuck, but in an attempt to get unstuck he dislodges some of the rocks and more of them crumble down upon him. Now, neither can he get himself out nor can you or your team help him.

You know that there is a limited supply of air in the mine and that if you do not get your team out in a few hours, they will all die of suffocation. Suddenly one of your mates grabs your shoulder. You turn and see he is holding a stick of dynamite in his hand. He found it near one of the mine walls and says he is 100 percent confident that if you used the dynamite you could free everyone from the mine shaft. However doing so would also certainly kill the stuck man in the process. What would you do? Is it better to take one human life by your own action in order to save nineteen others? Or is it better to not actively take one person's life, even if it indirectly results in the deaths of many more? In classroom discussions, professors may fuel the fire by asking, "What if the trapped man is your father?" or "What if he is a convicted murderer?" but the basic dilemma is the same.

There are two classic responses to the situation. The first is utilitarian. The utilitarian ethical thing to do is to act in a way to achieve an outcome that is the greatest good for the greatest number of people. In other words, light the dynamite, duck and cover. If the first classic response is utilitarian, the second is Kantian, after Immanuel Kant. Kant believed that ethics was about duties and that to be ethical you must fulfill your duties. This begs the question, What are your duties? Kant says that your duties derive from a demanding standard that he calls the "categorical imperative." In Kant's system, the categorical imperative is the supreme law by which all other ethics are derived. It is the ultimate commandment of reason from which all other duties emanate. So what is the categorical imperative? There are actually a couple different ways to put it. One is, "Act only according to that maxim whereby you can at the same time will that it should become a universal law." A second is, "Act in such a way that you treat humanity, whether in your own person or in the person of any other, always at the same time as an end and never merely as a means to an end."[2] In other words, you do not kill the fat man in the rubble because that would be treating him as a means to an end instead of an end in himself.

So what is it going to be? Do the ends justify the means? You kill the man but save the group. Or do the means justify the ends? The group dies, but you are not guilty of taking someone's life. Which is right? Reasonable people disagree. So where does that leave us? What good is it to pledge to be ethical if we cannot agree on what is the right thing to do? We cannot pretend to mediate correctly all ethical scenarios. But we do believe that there are certain standards that can be applied, along with knowledge of context and factors, to guide a manager's decisions.

We have been asked many times what the MBA Oath means by the promise to act "ethically." Our initial response is simple: it is to act the opposite of what people mean when they say MBAs are unethical. When people call MBAs "unethical," what do they mean? They probably mean they think MBAs act unfairly and will lie to and cheat whoever crosses their paths. Therefore, an imperfect, but workable, definition of what it means for MBAs to act ethically is the reverse of that: "Don't lie and don't cheat." Columbia Business School has adopted this view in an honor pledge for students that they "will not lie, cheat, or steal, or tolerate those who do." Yet even this straightforward command is hard to keep. Just think about how hard it was for those Coca-Cola executives to balance their customers' conceptions of fairness with their goal of charging what the market would bear for a beverage.

Fairness and "the MBA Mind"

A fundamental orienting concept in establishing what we mean by ethics and integrity is *fairness*. Employees want to earn a *fair wage*. Customers want a *fair price*. Investors want a *fair return*. The public doesn't want unfair tax breaks for big business. Business owners want other firms in their industry to compete fairly. Nations want fair trade. We can all agree that we support fairness. It is harder to agree on what fairness actually *is*. As a result, unions and managers haggle over wages. Customers bemoan prices they think are too high. Advocacy groups rail against lobbying behaviors of firms they think are getting unfair treatment. Business leaders complain and sometimes sue their competitors for tactics they think violate the principles of fair business. And thirsty customers get upset about whether or not vending machine prices are fair.

During our first year at business school, our entire class took a simple six-question quiz as part of a lesson on how differently people think about fairness. Each question described a scenario and asked you to decide whether it was fair or unfair. The quiz is actually quite well known. Our professors borrowed it from Princeton behavioral economist Daniel Kahneman, a Nobel Prize winner who may be the world's foremost expert on the topic of fairness. Kahneman has had thousands of people in the general public take the test. Our professors wanted to compare the outcomes for our MBA class to those found by Kahneman.[3] The results are revealing.

Before telling you what we learned, why don't you take the quiz yourself? That way you can compare your results with Kahneman's and with Harvard MBAs. It should only take a minute or two. Just mark down what you feel most deeply.

The Fairness Quiz

1. Hardware Store

A hardware store has been selling shovels for $15. The morning after a large snowstorm, the store raises the prices to $20. Please rate this action as

❑ Completely fair   ❑ Acceptable   ❑ Unfair   ❑ Very unfair

2. Elmo Auction

A store has been sold out of the popular Tickle Me Elmo dolls for a month. A week before Christmas, a single doll is discovered in the storeroom. The managers know that many customers would like to buy the doll. They announce over the store's public address system that the doll will be sold by auction to the customer who offers to pay the most. Please rate this action as

❏ Completely fair   ❏ Acceptable   ❏ Unfair ❏ Very unfair

3. Elmo and UNICEF

What if the store managers faced the same situation with the Tickle Me Elmo doll being sold out and decided to hold an auction, but instead of keeping the money themselves, they would donate the proceeds of the sale to UNICEF (The United Nations Children's Fund)?

❏ Completely fair   ❏ Acceptable   ❏ Unfair ❏ Very unfair

4. Lettuce Shortage

Due to a transportation mix-up, there is a local shortage of lettuce and the wholesale price has increased. A local grocer has purchased the usual quantity of lettuce at a price that is 30 cents (per head of lettuce) higher than normal. The grocer raises the price of lettuce to customers by 30 cents per head. Please rate this action as

❏ Completely fair   ❏ Acceptable   ❏ Unfair ❏ Very unfair

5. Grocery Chain

Speaking of groceries, imagine a grocery chain has stores in many communities. Most of them face competition from other grocery stores. In one community, the chain has no competition. Although its costs and volume of sales are the same there as elsewhere, the chain sets prices that average 5 percent higher than in other communities. Please rate this action as

❏ Completely fair ❏ Acceptable ❏ Unfair ❏ Very unfair

6. Landlord

A landlord rents out a small house. When the lease is due for renewal, the landlord learns that the tenant has taken a job very close to the house and is therefore unlikely to move. The landlord raises the rent $40 more per month than he was planning to do. Please rate this action as

❏ Completely fair ❏ Acceptable ❏ Unfair ❏ Very unfair

Finished? Now remember your answers and look at the results of the formal study duplicated below. This chart compares responses of the general public with those of MBAs. For each question, it reports the percentage of respondents from each group who answered either "completely fair" or "acceptable." How do your answers compare?

	% of respondents who answered "completely fair" or "acceptable"	
	GENERAL PUBLIC	MBAs
1. Hardware Store Snow Shovels	18%	75%
2. Elmo Auction	26%	63%
3. Elmo and UNICEF	79%	89%
4. Lettuce Shortage	79%	97%
5. Grocery Chain	24%	82%
6. Landlord	9%	40%

When asked whether a hardware store was justified in raising snow shovel prices after a snowstorm, 75 percent of our classmates said the action was either "completely fair" or "acceptable." Only 18 percent of the public agreed. Sixty-three percent of my classmates said holding an auction for Elmo dolls was "completely fair" or "acceptable." Only 26 percent of the public agreed. When the proceeds from the Elmo auction went to UNICEF more MBAs supported it (89 percent), but the charitable donation made an even bigger difference for the public. A full 79 percent of the public found the auction acceptable if the store wasn't profiting from it. In the lettuce scenario, the general public and MBAs are more or less on the same page. Most people agreed that a grocer has the right to raise her prices by the amount that her costs increase. On the second grocery store question we find wide disagreement between the public and MBAs. Eighty-two percent of MBAs thought the grocery stores could charge higher prices in the absence of competition. However, only a quarter of the general public agreed. The average person thinks this is price gouging. The landlord was the only situation among the six that a majority of MBAs found "unfair." Sixty percent of MBAs thought the landlord was acting unfairly and 91 percent of the public agreed. Still, even on this question there is a wide spread between MBA and the rest of the public.

So what about the difference between MBAs and the general public? A few things are worth noting. First, in each of the six scenarios, MBAs are more comfortable than the general public with the price increase in question. Second, a majority of MBAs thought the action in question was fair in every scenario except the "Landlord" scenario. By contrast, a majority of the public found four of the six scenarios unfair. Third, the differences between the opinions of MBAs and the general public tend to be large. In every scenario except the third (Elmo and UNICEF), there is at least a 30 percent gap between the two groups.

This survey suggests there is an "MBA mind" that differs from the "public mind" when it comes to fairness. The MBA mind believes raising prices is acceptable in cases where most other people would strongly disagree. What accounts for the difference? Why do MBAs believe it is acceptable to raise shovel prices in a snowstorm when the general public thinks such an action is unfair?

The easy conclusion is that MBAs are greedy, and the public is altruistic. MBAs want to raise prices and get rich whereas the general public is more generous. This is too simplistic. Another way to interpret the results is to assume that everyone is thinking in terms of their own self-interest, and the public is just as motivated by their self-interest as the MBAs are. It explains a lot if you assume that most members of the general public answer the quiz from the perspective of a *consumer* whereas most MBAs probably answer the questions from the standpoint of a *business manager*. Thus, in each of the six scenarios, the most financially advantageous answer for the consumer is to reject the price increase while the financial interests of the business manager will be best served by the price increases. As long as both groups approach the questions from their own perspectives they will remain wedded to their short-term financial interests, and they will come to opposite conclusions about what the "right" action is. Where you stand depends on where you sit.

John Rawls Attends a Wedding

Philosopher John Rawls concluded by means of logic the same thing that Daniel Kahneman discovered empirically in the fairness quiz: where you stand on an issue depends on where you sit. For example, the rich tend to want lower taxes and the poor tend to want a progressive tax on the rich to redistribute wealth to the poor. To compensate for these situation-dictated perspectives, Rawls contends we should imagine a hypothetical scenario that removes our prejudice. He says that we can only find justice if we stand behind a "veil of ignorance" where "no one knows his place in society, his class position or social status, nor does anyone know his fortune in the distribution of natural assets and abilities, his intelligence, strength, and the like." Rawls claims that only when we cease considering these details about our own situations will we be able to make judgments that are fair for all. You would be more likely to make a fair judgment if you have to make the judgment without knowing whether you are the boss, the employee, the shareholder, or the customer.

To make this more practical, let us consider a real scenario. A friend was getting married a couple of years ago. She made arrangements for the church, the flowers, the DJ. She rented a banquet hall at a hotel and sent invitations to her relatives and closest friends. It was to be the happiest day of her life. Then, just a few weeks before the wedding, a member of her immediate family died. It was a shock, an unexpected and devastating loss. She had to cancel the wedding.

Now imagine that you are the manager of the hotel and a good deal of your revenue is derived from hosting weddings in your ballroom. You are on the hook to meet monthly and quarterly sales targets. This wedding puts you safely in the black. Then you receive a call from the bride, saying she needs to cancel. What do you do? Do you refund her money? You probably feel conflicted. You feel bad for her and want to give her a full refund. You can justify this either by thinking it is a long-term strategy to keep your hotel's good reputation or by deciding it's just *the right thing to do*. On the other hand, you are not sure your boss in the corporate office will be as sympathetic. Maybe you have missed your sales goals for the last two quarters and you know your annual reviews are coming up. You know it is too late to find anyone else to book the ballroom for that weekend. Do you charge for the wedding, which will probably help your career? Or do you show sympathy to the bride and cancel the bill?

From another perspective, what if you were the employee who was scheduled to work overtime that night, pouring drinks and serving cake? Maybe you were counting on the extra income to pay for your child's birthday present. What would you want to happen? What will it tell you about your manager when he explains why he did or did not refund the money? What if you were the bride? The point is, Rawls would say you need to take all of these individuals' situations into account as you decide what the right thing to do is. In the case of my friend, the hotel manager refunded her money in full. She was so impressed that when it was time to reschedule the wedding she had no doubt as to which hotel she would give her business.

As we have seen, fairness is not a simple goal to achieve. Coca-Cola learned that the hard way. However, if we place ourselves "behind the veil of ignorance" (as John Rawls would counsel) or simply "put ourselves in the other guy's shoes" (as our grandparents might advise), we can improve our fairness batting percentage. This is one strategy, and a good one, we feel, for dealing with difficult ethical scenarios where the answers are not clear.

On Cheating

Woody Allen once said, "I was thrown out of college for cheating on the metaphysics exam; I looked into the soul of the boy sitting next to me." Recently Donald McCabe found that Woody was not the only one cheating. McCabe and his colleagues collected survey responses from 5,331 students at thirty-two graduate schools in the United States and Canada. They found that 56 percent of graduate business students had cheated, compared with 47 percent of graduate students in nonbusiness programs. Newspapers ran headlines about how MBAs cheat more than other graduate students, and they were right, but the rates are not that far apart. The fact that nearly half of all graduate students across every discipline admit to cheating says something profound about the societal value, or lack thereof, we place on playing by the rules of the game.

Cheating of any kind is unacceptable, so why do MBAs do it? One of the study's authors suggested in an interview it was the cultural norm. Among MBA students, "there's . . . a perception that their peers cheat more in a business-school environment and that they'll be disadvantaged if they don't."[4] According to the research, the mindset of most MBAs—the bottom line—is to get the highest GPA possible, regardless of the means, because the students with the highest GPAs get the best shot at the six-figure jobs in pharmaceuticals, high tech, and finance.

It is relevant to note that we did not witness a culture of cheating in our business school experience. We may have been blind to it, but the culture at our school took academic integrity seriously. Still, there is little reason to doubt McCabe's general findings because the students themselves reported that they cheat. When you think about it, that is at least an honest admission. As Tuck School of Business professor Aine Donovan writes, "Philosophy students, by contrast, know that cheating is anathema to the profession and they understand the repercussions for violating that professional norm. That does not mean that they don't cheat—they may just be better at lying about it. They would be loath to tell you they cheat."[5] What is more disturbing—that MBAs cheat, or that they do not mind telling you about it? At most business schools, ethics is not a central focus, so maybe business students are less bothered about admitting their cheating. Perhaps they have been trained to think it is not that important.

MIT behavioral economist Dan Ariely has also studied cheating. He says that it is a mistake to believe there are two groups of people, "cheaters" and "noncheaters." Most people are honest by and large, but circumstances tempt them to deviate from their basic values. Ariely and his fellow researchers tempted a few thousand "honest" people to cheat in a set of scientifically controlled experiments at Harvard, MIT, Princeton, UCLA, and Yale. Participants in the study were asked to complete twenty math problems within a five-minute time limit. The researchers told participants they would be paid fifty cents for each correct response. In control groups, the researchers found that on average, the participants would correctly answer four problems out of twenty. But in experimental groups, the researchers would shred answer sheets before looking at them so that respondents knew that it was impossible for the researchers to know whether they had answered the questions correctly. Therefore when participants were asked how many questions they had gotten right they had the opportunity to lie and receive more money than they had legitimately earned. "On average," Ariely explains, "they claimed to have correctly solved two problems more than they knew they had (six rather than four). That is, given the chance, the majority of people cheated by about 50 percent."[6]

Ariely and his colleagues tried to understand how circumstances influenced the degree to which people cheat. They found that getting people to contemplate their own standards of honesty (by recalling the Ten Commandments or signing an honor code) eliminated cheating completely. They also found that if payment was given in poker chips, which were exchanged for cash a few seconds later, the average level of cheating more than doubled. Ariely concludes, "Most of us, when tempted, are willing to be a little dishonest, regardless of the risks. [I]t's clear that we have an incredible ability to rationalize our dishonesty and that justifying it becomes substantially easier when cheating is one step removed from cash."[7]

Cheating, it turns out, is widespread and, for most of us, fairly easy to justify. A Rotman School of Management professor named Chen-Bo Zhong conducted a study to find out why. His results ironically indicate that people become more unethical when they are given time to reflect on their decisions rather than acting from their gut. His study set up a game between two test subjects at a time. The subjects were supposed to interact with each other, and each had the opportunity either to lie to the partner or to treat the partner fairly. If participants decided to act unfairly, they would gain at their partner's expense. Zhong gave each set of partners different rules for interaction. He told some of them to think rationally about the situation and decide what to do after careful deliberation, doing whatever they could to ignore their emotions. He told others that they should "trust their gut" and make decisions based primarily on their feelings.

Here is what he discovered. Sixty-nine percent of the "thinkers" decided to cheat their partners. The "gut feelers," on the other hand, chose to cheat only 27 percent of the time. The thinkers out-cheated the feelers by a wide margin. As Zhong puts it, "Deliberative processes can license morally questionable behaviors by focusing on tangible monetary outcomes and reducing emotional influence."[8] In other words, we can talk ourselves into doing what we know is wrong if the incentives are attractive enough.

We businesspeople are taught to trust our heads over our guts. We are taught to build cash flow models and to trust the models. We have an intuitive sense of what is right and wrong, just and unjust, fair and unfair. But anyone who has ever faced a situation where they could personally profit from doing the wrong thing knows how tempting it is to talk yourself out of what you know is right. You construct elaborate justifications and build towering arguments to convince yourself that your unrefined moral sense is not really faulty. You find a way to argue yourself into a belief that it is okay to bend the rules when it benefits you.

Let us state this frankly. The pure pursuit of self-interest does not create a true commitment to integrity or truth. Instances invariably arise when honesty arguably may not be in one's self-interest. Particularly when the risk of being discovered is low, the benefits of dishonesty can be tempting and seemingly serve one's self-interest. The problem arises when one justifies the little trespasses, and one day's minor trespass leads to the next. The justification becomes "I did it yesterday, so what difference does it make if I do it again today?" Jane Hamilton described the process in her novel *A Map of the World*:

> I used to think if you fell from grace it was more likely than not the result of one stupendous error, or else an unfortunate accident. I hadn't learned that it can happen so

gradually you don't lose your stomach or hurt yourself in the landing. You don't necessarily sense the motion. I've learned that it takes at least two and generally three things to alter the course of a life: you slip around the truth once, and then again, and one more time, and there you are, feeling, that it was sudden, your arrival at the bottom of the heap.[9]

As Hamilton warns, the process is insidious. The oath serves to remind and anchor as much as it serves to prod and motivate.

A provost from a business school went to Home Depot to buy a length of metal chain. He found the chain he wanted. It was on the bottom shelf, and when he looked at it, he could see that the price was $1.94 a foot. "I told the young man I wanted ten feet. And so, he went to measure it off and cut it. And then he wrote out the slip that I was to take up to the counter and he wrote $3.94. As soon as he wrote $3.94, I said, 'Wait a second, it's $1.94.'" The salesperson got down on his hands and knees, looked at the price tag, and apologized for the mistake, writing the correct price on the sheet.

"I proceeded to the cash register," the provost continued. "The cashier took the slip and she took the chain and entered it into the computer. 'Ninety-four cents a foot.' I had to think before I said anything. It scared me about myself because I consider myself an ethical person. I had no problem stopping the young man who was going to overcharge me, but I had to stop and think when they were going to undercharge me."[10] Sound like a familiar situation? The story strikes a chord because we have all been there. And many of us have not said anything to the cashier. It is their fault for being sloppy, we reason. We know it is wrong, but we make up justifications for our actions. We rationalize our own behavior.

We're Less Ethical Than We Think

Unlike the provost in the hardware store, we often fail to realize that we are making ethical compromises until it is too late. One of the major conclusions in the field of social psychology over the last fifty years is that people are less ethical than they think they are. By making small, "innocent" compromises, people fail to see the second- and third-order consequences and open the door to greater ethical trespasses. As Reinhold Niebuhr said, "The more we live with a necessary evil, the more necessary it seems and the less evil."

Some of the most famous and controversial experiments in the history of social science were conducted by Stanley Milgram at Yale in the 1960s and 1970s. Milgram was deeply troubled by the evils of Nazi Germany. His research question was, How can a nation of rational people allow such terrible evil? To explore this question, Milgram conducted a study on the phenomenon of obedience. In the experiment, he utilized volunteers to act as "teachers" who, unbeknownst to them, were the actual subjects of the experiment. The "teachers" were told that the experiment was intended to explore how punishment affects memory. In reality, the study was to test how much pain an ordinary citizen would inflict on another person simply because he was ordered to by an experimental scientist.

The volunteer teachers were asked to administer electrical shocks of increasing intensities to "learners" in an adjoining room when the learners made mistakes during the experiment.

The learners were actually actors who were not really shocked but pretended to react in discomfort as the teachers increased the level of the shocks. The experiment begins with the teacher delivering a 15-volt charge to the learner for the first mistake the learner makes. As the experiment goes on, the intensity of each shock increases by 15 volts with each mistake, all the way up to 450 volts. So the actors scream louder and louder, at one point complaining of heart palpitations, then begging to be released and yelling in agony. Then the actor, who is located out of sight in another room, goes silent. The volunteer teacher is left to wonder what happened. Did he pass out? Is he refusing to participate? Is he dead? If the volunteer asked the experimenter who was responsible for any harmful effects resulting from the electrical shocks, he was told that someone else—the experimenter—would assume full responsibility for any such harm. On that basis, the teachers continued to shock the students, shifting responsibility for their actions to another person and reduce their own felt responsibility for the outcome.

Despite the horrific circumstances, 60 percent of the teachers actually obeyed orders to shock students the maximum amount of voltage and no teacher stopped before reaching the 300-volt level. Milgram summarized his findings in an article stating,

> Stark authority was pitted against the subjects' [participants'] strongest moral imperatives against hurting others, and, with the subjects' [participants'] ears ringing with the screams of the victims, authority won more often than not. . . . Ordinary people, simply doing their jobs, and without any particular hostility on their part, can become agents in a terrible destructive process. Moreover, even when the

destructive effects of their work become patently clear, and they are asked to carry out actions incompatible with fundamental standards of morality, relatively few people have the resources needed to resist authority.[11]

Thus, Nazi death camp atrocities were justified by statements such as "I was just doing my job" or "I am only a small cog in machinery far greater than me." Milgram repeated his experiment thousands of times, with people from all walks of life in many different countries and cultures with the same or similar results.

Milgram's experiments also revealed that one of the factors affecting the outcome was *proximity of the victim*. Participants acted with least compassion when the "learners" could not be seen, and the learners could not see them. When the learner was remote, nearly all participants were fully obedient. When the learner was in the room, the obedience rate dropped to 40 percent. This has major implications for CEOs considering mass layoffs, or Wall Street executives risking the money of pensioners. If you are in a position of leadership and are considering an action that might cause harm, challenge yourself to be in a place where you have actual contact with the potential victims.

As part of our study of the Milgram experiments, our professors asked our class to anonymously answer two questions and turn them in. First, if you were one of the "teachers" in the experiment, at what voltage do you think your conscience would kick in and you would refuse to go further? Second, at what voltage do you think the average of the rest of the class would stop? Our professors compiled our answers. The results were humbling. Every single person in the class thought that they would stop at a lower voltage than the average of the class as a whole. In other words, every last one of us thought that we were more ethical and conscientious than our average classmate. By definition, it is impossible for us all to be above average. So at least half of us were kidding ourselves. More likely, every one of us was overconfident in our own ethicality.

We are tempted to reduce complicated ethical questions to black-and-white superficialities and to believe that there are "good guys" and "bad guys" in the world. We want to declare that Jeff Skilling and Bernard Madoff did not just make unethical decisions. We want to say they are a different breed of people. We want to categorize people and put them into buckets as either heroes or villains, angels or demons, without recognizing the awful truth that the good people aren't as good as we would like to think they are, and the bad people often are not quite as bad. Milgram's experiments confirm what Ariely found when studying cheating. They teach us that the truth is much trickier. In reality, we all have both good and evil inside of us. Aleksandr Solzhenitsyn described it this way: "[T]he line separating good and evil passes not through states, not between classes, not between political parties either—but right through every human heart and all human hearts. This line shifts. Inside us it oscillates with the years. And even within hearts overwhelmed by evil, one small bridgehead of good is retained. And even in the best of hearts there remains an uprooted small corner of evil."[12]

Most people who act unethically are not unethical through and through. They have spouses, children, and friends. They have high hopes and standards for their life. They have aspirations of living lives of integrity and goodness, but they get tripped up along the way. In other words, "they" are "us." An analyst has his boss breathing down his neck because her boss has put pressure on her. The boss is feeling the pressure from shareholders, and the quarterly numbers are due, so they'd better do something right. Hence, the analyst changes a number or two on a spreadsheet to smooth things over. No one finds out, so he does it again and then again. He is rewarded for his work and is promoted because no one noticed. But now he has set unrealistic expectations for the firm and for himself. In a high-pressure situation with time constraints and high stakes, you may feel pressure to conform to the "norm," not appear weak, and follow the example of those in positions of authority. All these factors can lead you to behave in ways that go against your own moral standards.

Reflecting on his own research and that of Milgram and others, Stanford social psychologist Philip Zimbardo concludes that human behavior is determined far more by contextual and situational forces than by individual character. In a match between group dynamics and inherent nature, group dynamics would win in a knockout. "Ethical problems in companies," he argues, "don't come from 'a few bad apples' but from 'the barrel makers,'—the leaders who, wittingly or not, create and maintain the systems in which participants are encouraged to do wrong."[13]

As leaders, we *must* understand that situation and context are enormously important. In fact, despite what we would like to believe, situation is a more powerful influence than character for most people. When you enter business school, it is likely you have never actually been in a position of authority before. You have been a consulting or banking analyst, but you took your marching orders from others rather than delivering them to someone else. It is easy for us to miss the fact that once you are in authority, people will often do what you say simply because you have authority. You may expect them to question you and check your judgment, but as Milgram found, most of the time, that does not happen.

How Then Shall We Lead?

After learning about Milgram's findings, it is tempting to lose hope, to conclude that we have no volition and that character is irrelevant. It is precisely because the influence of context and situations is so strong that it is so inspiring when we see examples of individuals rising above it. Nelson Mandela endured nearly three decades in prison and still found the strength to forgive his prison keepers. His fellow prisoners all say the strength of his character allowed them to rise above the influence of the horrific situation they were in, and specifically above the strong feelings of revenge to which most people would succumb. One individual with great strength of character can overcome a difficult situation, and can inspire others to do the same.

The mistake is to think that this is easy or to assume that you are somehow more capable of this than others are. Far better to assume that you will struggle like everyone else to clearly identify moral dilemmas, and that it will be difficult to act in a courageous and principled way. If Milgram, Ariely, and other researchers are right, we are all susceptible to moral blindness if the circumstances are right. Better to be skeptical about your own character and begin a plan to shore up your weaknesses. How do you do that? Here are a few suggestions.

First, make a commitment to do the small things right. A person's character, like one's garden, reflects the amount of weeding that was done in the growing season. Doing little things wrong opens the possibilities of doing big things wrong, therefore be strong even in the little things. When you make an oath of ethics and integrity, go all the way. Kill the weeds at the root level.

Second, use a more rigorous framework for decision making

than simply "whatever feels right," but do not ignore your gut instinct as you consider monetary outcomes of your decisions. Consider breaking down ethical decisions to their component parts of intention, means, and outcome. Consider to whom you are obliged, both inside and outside your organization, both now and in the future. Use the philosophical framework of thinkers like Rawls. Consciously doing these things will most likely lead us to better, more thoughtful decisions.

Third, become more self-aware. Recognize that your confidence in your own virtue may be misplaced. Understand that you may be compromised. You may say to yourself, "I would never cheat in a business deal. That's not the kind of person I am." Make room for self-doubt in statements like that and design around the possibility that you may be wrong. One way to design around your own weakness is to surround yourself with naysayers. As a manager, you need an unimpeded flow of information and a climate where no one fears punishment for speaking up. Instead of punishing people for being naysayers, you ought to reward them to reinforce moral courage among your employees. Jamie Dimon, the CEO of JPMorgan Chase, once sat on a discussion panel at which one of the other panelists said you need to have at least one person around you whom you can trust to tell you the truth. Dimon responded, "If you only have one person telling you the truth, you're in big trouble!"

The MBA Oath is a pledge to do whatever it takes to lead ethically and with integrity. Kate Barton is a classmate and co-leader of the MBA Oath. She put it like this: "It is the responsibility of business professionals to think more externally, more long-term, more broadly about the decisions we make and the people and systems we affect. The oath, to me, fills a gap in the current business education system by giving students and alumni the opportunity to take individual responsibility for their decisions, and commit to rising to a higher standard of ethics through the MBA Oath." If management is to be a profession, and if MBAs want to call themselves leaders, we must begin by committing to integrity and ethics. These are nonnegotiables.

7

NO MAN IS AN ISLAND

I will safeguard the interests of my shareholders, cowork-ers, customers, and the society in which we operate. I will endeavor to protect the interests of those who may not have power but whose well-being is contingent on my decisions.

MBA Oath, Second Promise

When I heard about the MBA Oath, I became lifted with the hope that the next generation of MBAs would do better than mine has, and that those of us who have come before can declare anew our commitment to true excellence: integrity, honor, and positive lasting contributions to our society.

Bill Hughes, MIT, Class of 1994, signer #1686

Toward the end of his life, the English poet John Donne wrote a meditation on the interconnectedness of man-kind and the necessity of looking out for one another.

No man is an island, entire of itself. Every man is a piece of the continent, a part of the main; if a clod be washed away by the sea, Europe is the less, as well as if a promontory were, as well as if a manor of thy friends or of thine own were: any

> man's death diminishes me, because I am involved in man-
> kind. Therefore never send to know for whom the bell tolls;
> it tolls for thee.

The second promise of the MBA Oath is a pledge to safeguard the interests of shareholders, coworkers, customers, and the society in which we operate. Business leaders must by necessity be concerned for the welfare of all four of these groups. As we will argue in this chapter, John Donne was right. "No man is an island." Similarly, no single stakeholder in a business is an island. All stakeholders are "a part of the main," and if a clod is washed to sea, the rest of a firm's stakeholders are the less for the loss. Recent experience has taught us that not only are the stakeholders of an individual firm dependent upon each other, but stakeholders of different firms are also interdependent. We ignore the systemic interrelations of the financial system at our own peril. The truth is, we are all in this together.

What does it mean to safeguard the interests of stakeholders? Is it code for taking from shareholders and giving to other groups? Are we suggesting that managers do not owe a special duty to shareholders? Absolutely not. So what do we mean? We mean that the leaders of businesses owe a duty to shareholders and must vigorously pursue that duty while at the same time working to satisfy the legitimate claims of the other stakeholders. This is the complicated, yet necessary, task of all managers.

Act I. Hometown Hero

Aaron Feuerstein was a hometown hero. His grandfather had founded the company, a fabric manufacturing plant, in the town of Malden, Massachusetts, in 1908. Ever since, Malden Mills and its leaders had been pillars of the community: self-made, but community-minded. When Malden Mills's chief product, fake fur, suddenly fell out of fashion in the 1980s, the company faced major financial trouble, but Aaron Feuerstein led the company's transformation with the creation of two new highly innovative and successful products—Polartec and Polarfleece. These performance fabrics, developed from recycled plastics, became wildly popular. Feuerstein was hailed as a visionary by employees and the local community.[1]

In the 1980s and 1990s, other garment makers left New England to relocate their operations closer to cotton in the South or where cheap labor was abundant overseas. Offshoring was becoming the norm, and it enabled huge cost savings for firms willing to close down their domestic divisions. While American workers earned close to seven dollars an hour, a Mexican worker would earn only one dollar an hour, and a worker in Asia could be paid less than a couple of dollars per day. Despite these cost advantages, Feuerstein chose to keep Malden Mills in its historic New England home. Its largest plant was in Lawrence, Massachusetts, one of the thirty poorest cities in the entire country. Feuerstein's firm was one of Lawrence's largest employers. If Malden Mills were to abandon its home in Lawrence, the entire community could collapse. Feuerstein felt a sense of duty and loyalty to the town. Unless circumstances changed drastically, workers in Lawrence could count on their jobs at Malden Mills.

Then in 1995, circumstances quickly and drastically did change. A freak accident sparked a fire at Malden's main plant. The facility was filled with highly flammable materials. Within hours the entire building was decimated. It was the largest fire in Massachusetts in a century. As a local reporter described it, "In a single evening, Malden Mills quite literally went up in smoke." The fire and its aftermath were devastating. It would cost the company millions of dollars, and town residents realized the broader implication of the fire: this was the end of garment production in New England. If Malden Mills rose from the ashes, it would have to do so in another part of the world, and the workers in Lawrence would need to find new jobs.

But Aaron Feuerstein surprised everyone. On the day after the fire, he made a remarkable speech in which he committed to give all three thousand Malden Mills employees full pay and benefits for three months, regardless of whether they returned to the company. Second, he committed to continuing a program he started to help workers buy their first homes. Third, and most astonishing, he announced that he would rebuild the plant in Lawrence instead of moving operations overseas.

People were stunned. The public was accustomed to cost-slashing CEOs who were cold to the human toll of their layoffs. Here was a man who boldly moved against the current. He actually cared about the community. He actually cared about his employees. Who would think that a CEO with compassion and vision like that existed? Feuerstein was a hero. President Clinton met with him and invited him as a guest to the State of the Union speech. He was featured in *People* magazine. Twelve universities gave him honorary degrees. Secretary of Labor Robert Reich proclaimed, "This is what every CEO in America ought to be doing."[2] The story should have ended like a Hollywood movie, and the credits should have rolled with not a dry eye in the theater.

It was not to be. Rebuilding the plant cost more than Feuerstein anticipated, by millions of dollars. Moreover, one of the divisions ran into complications rebuilding and had to be shut down, after Malden spent $50 million on the construction. Unbranded fleece producers began to cut into Polarfleece's market share, reducing Malden's anticipated sales. Problems mounted and so did the financial distress. Eventually it became obvious that Malden Mills would not be able to pay the interest on its loans. In the fall of 2001, five years after the fire, Malden Mills filed for bankruptcy. Feuerstein's gambit to save the company and the town had failed.

Many people remember Aaron Feuerstein's compassion and courage. Few recall the price he paid for his heroics. His story reminds us of the complexity of the matrix in which we exist. While attending to the needs of one group of stakeholders, his employees, Feuerstein's actions failed to protect and preserve the interests of other stakeholders—the company shareholders and creditors. Feuerstein had received $300 million in insurance coverage for the fire. When a reporter suggested that he should have taken the money and been happy instead of trying to rebuild, Feuerstein snorted, "And what would I do with it? Eat more? Buy another suit? Retire and die?"[3]

Feuerstein's zeal and compassion for his employees is laudable. No doubt he was a man with a larger than average sized heart. His experience, however, demonstrates that as a manager, heart alone is not enough. In the MBA Oath, we commit to safeguard the interests of four groups of stakeholders—shareholders, employees, customers, and the public. We contend that if a manager overfocuses on one of the four groups, he will ultimately fail. Feuerstein overfocused on his employees and neglected to safeguard his investors. The decision cost him his company.

Our pledge is to run our enterprises well by safeguarding the interests of *all* stakeholders. Others will argue that they have a simpler solution: just safeguard the interests of shareholders and you need not worry about the rest. However, if we take that strategy to its logical extreme, it too will fail. Would we really support a business that provides value to its owners but not to its customers, employees, or society? Could such a business even exist?

Ben Edelman, a professor at Harvard Business School, may have found such a business. He is an Internet expert on the topic of spyware: how it is installed, how it makes money, and what can be done to combat it. If you have ever been frustrated with an infestation of spyware on your computer, Ben Edelman is fighting on your side. Most Internet users rightly complain about spyware because of the serious effects on their privacy and productivity. Pop-up ads not only annoy, they also are evidence that your behavior is being tracked and stored on central servers, building an ever-growing profile of who you are. Ben Edelman has discovered that some spyware vendors have found a way to exploit online affiliate advertising and give nothing of value in return.

An online affiliate advertising program allows you to make money by referring visitors on your blog or Web site to another commercial site. For instance, you could join Amazon.com's affiliate marketing program and publish on your Facebook page a link to our book on Amazon's Web site. If one of your friends clicks the link and buys the book, not only will you make us happy, you will earn a small finder's fee for yourself from Amazon.

Some spyware programs have discovered a way to exploit these programs. For example, say you like movies and decide you want to become a customer of Blockbuster online. You open your browser and type in "Blockbuster." Unbeknown to you, a secretly installed spyware program running in the background on your computer recognizes your search and hijacks the request, generating a full-screen pop-up that appears to be the official Blockbuster site.

It looks just like your browser window, so you might not realize what has happened. When you click a link on the pop-up, you are directed to the real Blockbuster site to sign up for an account. Blockbuster's computers recognize that you came through a third-party link (the pop-up link) and therefore credits the spyware firm (they have set up an affiliate account) with a finder's fee, maybe fifteen dollars per new customer. Blockbuster's computers fail to realize that the spyware software basically stole the natural search traffic Blockbuster would have received, and charged Blockbuster for redirecting them. The owners of the spyware company made a lot of money, but they gave nothing in return to anyone else. They gave nothing to their "customer," Blockbuster—you would have visited Blockbuster's site anyway. They gave nothing to society, you the involuntary user—except slowing down your computer by running in the background. They are parasites. They make profits, but they fail to create value.

As this example demonstrates, creating value for owners alone is insufficient justification for a business. Those who take the MBA Oath are called to create value for all stakeholders without overemphasizing any single group. How is this done? The story of another industrialist about five hours south of Malden Mills offers a clue.

Act II. Safeguarding

In 1987, when Paul O'Neill became CEO of Alcoa, the company was the largest aluminum producer in the United States. Yet Alcoa was not on particularly strong financial footing. Industry analysts and competitors watched carefully to see what O'Neill's first moves would be to stabilize the industrial giant. They were expecting something clearly focused on the bottom line: increasing sales, expanding to new markets, making the smelting process more cost-effective. They were more than a little surprised when he announced his top priority. O'Neill said his focus would be . . . safety.

Safety? This hardly made sense. First, O'Neill was not known to be a touchy-feely manager. In his previous job at International Paper he was known for his relentless schedule and for demanding results. Second, although safety was certainly a concern—aluminum is a dangerous industry—Alcoa had the best safety record in the business and had already halved its rate of serious injuries over the previous ten years. The rate of time that Alcoa employees lost to injury was only one-third the U.S. average.[4] In other words, O'Neill's strategy to save the rust belt manufacturer was to improve on something the company was already good at, and which was only indirectly related to its financial performance.

Still, O'Neill believed that by making safety the goal, *every* employee could directly play a part in improving the company. After all, safety was in everyone's interests. *Every man is a piece of the continent, a part of the main.* Alcoa workers suffered more than two thousand serious injuries the year O'Neill took control. He wanted the number of injuries to drop to zero. He declared that no one at Alcoa should ever be hurt at work. "If anyone ever calculates how much money we're saving by being safe, they're fired."[5] For Paul O'Neill, safety was not just a priority. It was a cardinal rule.

His strategy paid off. Alcoa's rate of time lost because of employee injuries was one-third the U.S. average when O'Neill took over. When he left, it was less than one-twentieth. Not only did Alcoa become one of the safest companies in the world, regardless of industry, it also became incredibly financially successful. In 1986, the Pittsburgh-based company recorded $264 million in net income on sales of $4.6 billion with 35,700 employees. When O'Neill retired fourteen years later, Alcoa boasted record profits of $1.5 billion on sales of $22.9 billion and a payroll of 140,000 persons.[6]

Paul O'Neill's commitment to safety, of all things, became the hallmark of his leadership. O'Neill's safety commitment won over labor unions and in the process taught employees the value of meeting benchmarks and managing with metrics, skills that could be translated from measuring safety to measuring quality and efficiency. His benchmarks were later expanded to include financial results. O'Neill took care of his employees, and his employees took care of the company. O'Neill's story is interesting precisely because it is so unusual. O'Neill, like Feuerstein, focused on employees, but unlike Feuerstein, he did not focus on employees exclusively. Although he safeguarded their interests, he also kept his hand on the dial to protect shareholder interests and the bottom line. He understood that the manner in which he built employee morale would, in the long run, ensure employee loyalty as well as garner quality and quantity in production.

Balancing the interests of various stakeholders is not as easy as O'Neill made it look. Consider the following scenario, posted by a *New York Times* writer who read our oath and wanted to explore what it meant to safeguard the interests of employees.

You run a small business and learn that your CFO is the wrong person for the job. You interview candidates for weeks but can't find someone who has all the skills you require. Eventually your bank gets impatient and threatens to call your loan if you do not get someone in the role. So you hire the best candidate you saw— someone who was not bad but who is not exactly what you were looking for either. He quits his current job and plans to start in a few weeks.

The next week your bank calls to say they found the perfect candidate for you. You explain you already hired someone. The banker's tone changes from relief to concern. He asks you to just meet the person. You do, and it is true—she is exactly the candidate you wanted. She can solve your problems and can take you far beyond them. The writer explains the dilemma:

> You want to cry. You want to hug your mother. You are also sick to your stomach. What about the guy you've already hired? . . . The guy who got a "good" reference but nothing like the praise that was heaped on Super Woman. The guy who has already quit his job.
>
> Your banker says these things happen: Hire the woman! Your accountant agrees. You talk to your spouse. You talk to your best friend. They both are horrified that you would consider taking back your offer. Even your dog seems surprised.[7]

What do you do? It is a tough question. If you want to "safeguard the interests of employees," does this mean that you take the riskier option of sticking with the CFO candidate that you just hired or do you back out of that agreement in the interest of the bank, the shareholders, and the company? Our friend Dan replied with this comment:

> This case is similar to a situation where you went to a dance with a nice girl only to see a gorgeous girl outside the dance, and we're tempted by the "what-ifs" of being with the prettier girl. But what happens if you ditch your date and switch? Maybe nothing, and you have a great party. But in a world of potential repeated encounters, maybe your original date gets upset and tells her friends (making it harder to get future dates) or makes your life difficult (sues you

for making her quit her job for nothing—yes, the analogy is stretched here). What if the gorgeous girl saw you ditch your date for her? Might she think twice about going with you? Or worse, maybe she has no problem with going with you, but she'll ditch you the same way when that triathlete billionaire walks around the corner in five minutes.

The point? Commitments matter and are the foundation for good relationships (both personal and professional). Rescinding an offer in the manner proposed in the case brings serious reputational risk as well as inviting similar treatment/expectations, which could hurt the company in the long-term. I could see "right" outcomes with the original candidate and also without him. However, the way this decision is reached does matter.[8]

There is a power asymmetry between managers and employees, one that managers need to deal with appropriately. As managers, we have the power to provide jobs or replace employees with technology, the power to shape working conditions and people's futures. We need to balance the hard economics of labor costs with the soft economics of fairness, morale, and mutual commitment. This balance is important because, as O'Neill's case demonstrates, employees are more likely to engage in discretionary behavior to benefit the organization if they trust their supervisors to treat them fairly and perceive their organization to operate fairly. As Starbucks Founder Howard Schultz describes, "Our mission statement about treating people with respect and dignity is not just words but a creed we live by every day. You can't expect your employees to exceed the expectations of your customers if you don't exceed the employees' expectations of management."

Safeguarding the interests of employees is not simple to

explain. It does not mean "not firing anyone," because sometimes the best thing to do for the majority of employees is to eliminate the ones who are bringing down the group. A signer of the MBA Oath will of course occasionally have to fire employees, but how he or she does it matters—for him or her as an individual, for the employee, and for the company.

In a study of wrongful termination lawsuits, Allan Lind, Jerald Greenberg, Kimberly S. Scott, and Thomas D. Welchans found an overwhelming correlation between how employees felt they were treated and whether they pursued legal action. They interviewed hundreds of employees who had been terminated and found that whether employees felt that they were treated fairly, treated with dignity and respect, or given an explanation for the termination made all the difference in determining whether the employees decided to sue their former employer.

Percent of terminated employees pursuing wrongful termination claims. List sorted by employees' self-reports of how they were treated when they were fired.[9]

	(HIGH/VERY MUCH)	(LOW/NOT AT ALL)
Treated with fairness	0.9%	20.6%
Treated with dignity and respect	0.4%	15%
Given an explanation	1.8%	19.5%

The results are impossible to ignore. One out of five employees who do not feel like they were treated with fairness, respect, or given an explanation for their firing initiate a lawsuit against their employer. On the other hand, almost none of those who were given an explanation and who felt treated fairly and with respect initiated legal claims. Managers forced into the difficult position of terminating employees should remember those statistics and safeguard the interests of their employees even as they are letting them go.

We had the opportunity to hear Paul O'Neill speak a couple years ago, after he had left Alcoa and served as U.S. Treasury secretary. When asked why he had focused on safety, of all things, and what his philosophy of management was, he stated: "Over the course of my career in business and with the government, I have come to believe that people need three things to be happy in their jobs. Each person needs to be treated with dignity and respect at all times; each needs the tools to make a meaningful contribution to his or her organization; and each person needs to be recognized for the contributions that he or she makes." O'Neill's success at Alcoa is a powerful demonstration of how those principles are good not just for employees but also for the firm. No man is an island, not even the CEO.

Act III. Rapid Response

In 2004, the second-largest earthquake on record hit in the middle of the Indian Ocean. The quake caused a tsunami that struck Southeast Asia. The massive waves killed more than two hundred thousand people and displaced millions from their homes. It was Christmastime. We remember watching the tragedy unfold on TV with our families. Immediately there were reports of governments providing aid. Organizations like the Red Cross and World Vision went to the front lines, providing rescues, assistance, and rebuilding. Around the world, private citizens participated by donating money and supplies to campaigns through churches, aid agencies, and communities. Equally as inspiring as

this outpouring of global citizenship were the actions of Fritidsresor, one of Sweden's leading tour operators, in the wake of the
calamity. The company's response was heroic and is a good illus-
tration of balancing incredibly complex stakeholder interests.[10]

Fritidsresor plans vacations for Scandinavians to travel around
the world. One of its most popular destinations is Thailand. In
fact, at the time of the tsunami, Fritidsresor knew of ten thousand to fifteen thousand Swedish tourists in Thailand. It also had
hundreds of employees in the affected region. Imagine you are
the CEO of that company. You get a call at four in the morning
telling you that there is a catastrophe in a distant part of the
world. What do you do? Whose interests do you seek to protect?
How do you prioritize? The company's customers in Thailand?
The company's employees? Anyone else? What is an acceptable
way to spend shareholder money?

Fritidsresor was not in a position to waste money. The company had lost $32 million in 2003. Any impulse to spend money
searching for employees and customers would be tempered by
its shrinking accounts. Moreover, Fritidsresor's business would
be further devastated when its future customers canceled their
upcoming trips to Southeast Asia. Amid the panic, many companies would feel paralyzed. Who would blame Fritidsresor if it left
the search and rescue to the authorities?

Managers have a wide range of action-guiding principles for
managing externalities, the unintentional consequences of doing
business.[11] In a situation like this, consider six possible options
for action:

Level 1: Do not do harm
Level 2: Do not benefit from harm

Level 3: Compensate for harm

Level 4: Prevent harm

Level 5: Remove harm

Level 6: Do or promote good

As much as possible, we ought to internalize the costs of externalities. As signers of the MBA Oath, we think that managers ought to make it their baseline to operate at level 1 and make it their ambition to operate at level 6. Fritidsresor turns out to be one of the rare firms that in the wake of the tsunami pursued a level 6 response.

When the CEO received a call about the calamity at 4:00 a.m. on Christmas, he took the call and set his team in motion to respond to the crisis. In the moment of decision, with human lives at stake, there was no question for Fritidsresor's CEO about what the right thing to do was. His firm would do what it could both to find and rescue its customers and to support ongoing rescue efforts for all who were affected.

Having anticipated the potential for major catastrophes like the tsunami, the company already had emergency systems in place. They trusted and used the systems, focusing on people and safety first. Because of its experience in the region, Fritidsresor was also able to provide accurate and timely information to the government and donated the use of its emergency communication system to locate non-Fritidsresor travelers who were missing. One of the toughest challenges of management is to define and prioritize a company's stakeholders. In this instance, Fritidsresor succeeded in an admirable way. As a result, the company won the respect and admiration of the public, and no small amount of loyalty from its own customers.

In this chapter, we have seen complicated examples from Malden Mills, Alcoa, and Fritidsresor of how to balance the interests of stakeholders. As signers of the MBA Oath, our call is to safeguard the interests of shareholders, employees, customers, and the society in which we operate. The trade-offs are difficult. There is some wisdom in what Milton Friedman wrote about businesses not getting involved in trying to save the world. Aaron Feuerstein's experience with Malden Mills proves it. So how should a manager decide when to intervene and when not to?

In business school, we learned four insightful questions to help determine what responsibilities we owe to third parties in distress: connection, vulnerability, seriousness, and the ability and authority to change. Peter Drucker said that the single biggest source of mistakes in management decision making is the search for the right answer rather than the right question. In that spirit, we offer these four questions that can serve as a decision-making aid:[12]

How strong is our connection to the injury or harm? To what extent have our actions caused or contributed to the harm? How much are we benefitting from the harm? How much do we control or influence the harm? Do we have unique or special expertise to bear on the harm?

How vulnerable are the parties at risk? Are the affected parties able to contend with the situation? Are they free to act? Do they have access to information? Do they have viable avenues of recourse?

How serious is the injury or harm? What is the nature of the injury or harm? Does it involve basic human rights, health, safety, life? What is the scope of the injury or harm?

Do we have the ability and the authority from our investors, the public, others to address the situation?

The stronger the connection, the more vulnerable the parties at risk, the more serious the harm, the greater ability and authority the firm has to respond, then the greater responsibility the firm has to respond. Aaron Feuerstein's answer to the first three questions above was "very." The connection was strong—the fire happened at the plant. The parties were vulnerable—they had few other options for jobs. The harm was serious. However, Feuerstein did not have the *ability* to compensate for the harm, at least not the way he wanted to. He might have chosen to continue to pay the employees for six months, but close the factory. He could not afford to pay them, give them the home loans, and rebuild in the same town. Fritidsresor, on the other hand, was in a different situation. They had the *ability* to respond to crisis and they proactively did what was necessary to make the change.

═════

No man is an island. The same is true for any company. Managers seeking to reconcile the interests of shareholders, coworkers, customers, and society will likely encounter conflicts and be forced to make difficult choices. The danger lies in focusing myopically on a particular stakeholder to the detriment of the rest. When this happens, when managers take their eyes off the Richter scale, they will be surprised when the tectonic plates of various stakeholder interests collide and disrupt the organizations they have been trying to protect and grow.

8

AMBITION AND GOOD FAITH

I will manage my enterprise in good faith, guarding against decisions and behavior that advance my own narrow ambitions but harm the enterprise and the people it serves.

MBA Oath, Third Promise

My hope and goal is to help create a new movement of ethical MBAs who are not only concerned with being successful but also who are cognizant of the impact of their decisions on society as a whole. Let's take away the perception of MBAs as greedy individuals who are only concerned with making money.

Garen Grigoryan, Golden Gate University, MBA 2009,
signer #1759

One of the most memorable cases we studied at business school was not about business at all, but about a man on an arduous trek in the Himalayas.[1] The man was Bowen McCoy, a managing director at Morgan Stanley. During a sabbatical, McCoy and a friend decided to travel to the Himalayas for several weeks to trek through hundreds of miles of trails in some of the most remote and beautiful terrain on earth. The high point of their hike was an eighteen-thousand-foot pass they had to traverse in order to reach an isolated and beautiful village on the other side. This trip was a once-in-a-lifetime opportunity, and if they failed to make it over the pass, they would never see the village.

The pass was also the most dangerous part of their trek. They had already failed to cross the pass once because the trail was icy and the snow hip deep. This attempt would be their last chance. However, even with good weather, the altitude alone posed a significant physical challenge. Six years earlier, in another part of the world, McCoy had suffered pulmonary edema, an acute form of altitude sickness, at an elevation lower than this. He and his friend were concerned.

The morning that they were to make their ascent up and over the pass, a strange thing happened. A barely clothed *sadhu,* an Indian holy man, came staggering down the path from the pass and collapsed just ahead of McCoy and his group. It was a surreal encounter and it raised a host of questions. *What was this man doing all alone? Why was he nearly naked? Shouldn't he be more responsible for himself?* The sadhu was clearly sick, physically exhausted from climbing over the pass, and frostbitten by the elements. McCoy and his companions did not know if the man would survive.

The climbers debated about what to do. Would they give up the climb and get the stranger help? Would they leave the man and continue the climb? Precious minutes passed. The ascent had to be made before sundown. The group was already behind schedule. McCoy made a snap decision. He announced that he was leaving to get over the ridge to reach the town as planned. Another group of hikers was not far behind, he argued. Let them take care of the man. McCoy's friend was shocked. It was irresponsible. The man could die. He said he would stay with the sadhu until another group arrived that could give him proper medical attention. An icy look passed between McCoy and his friend. McCoy said they would meet on the other side.

Hours later, McCoy's friend finally arrived at the tent on the other side of the ridge. He was visibly disturbed. In order to catch up with McCoy, he had been forced to leave the sadhu prematurely before ensuring he would survive. They left him on the side of the mountain and hoped some group with more time than they had could provide care to the man. Neither McCoy nor his friend ever found out if the sadhu survived.

When Sir Edmund Hillary was asked why he wanted to climb Mt. Everest, Hilary replied, "Because it was there." Mountains call us to climb. The trek may be difficult, even dangerous, but we know there is a reward in reaching the peak. Many covet the mountaintop experience so much they are willing to risk their lives to get there. It is a dangerous business. For every eleven people who make it to the top of Everest, another climber dies trying. Because of the danger, over time, climbers have developed a code of the mountain: it is more important to get down the mountain than it is to get to the top. Experienced climbers know the risks involved and consider it a duty to help others who are struggling along the way. Yet not everyone follows the code. Sometimes the siren song of the summit is impossible to resist. It happened to Bowen McCoy. He had one blinding vision—to make it over the pass—and nothing was going to stop him. Not the weather, not the altitude, and not a man dying at his feet.

Though the heights of the Himalayas are far removed from the factory floor, the story of the sadhu is a parable that has profound lessons for business. The social and emotional dynamics of climbing a mountain are not so different from climbing the corporate ladder. A corporate manager is on a mission to achieve some *thing*, and he is so devoted to it, he neglects his responsibility to his companions. They encounter an issue together, but he takes the easy way out for himself and leaves them to deal with it alone. Ambition will get you up the mountain or up the ladder, but that same ambition may tempt you to step on or over anyone who gets in your way. Ambition creates in us a dual capacity for both personal achievement and interpersonal indifference.

The third promise of the MBA Oath is about resolving the problem of ambition. It calls us to manage our enterprises in good faith, with loyalty and care, guarding against decisions and behavior that advance our own narrow ambitions but harm our enterprises and the people they serve. The oath recognizes that pursuing one's self-interest is a foundation of capitalism and is a good thing, but it refuses to naively go one step further and justify greed.

In this chapter, we look at ambition from three angles: the altruism of ambition, the amnesia of ambition, and the aspiration of ambition. We see how ambition can be good, how it can corrupt, and how we need to act in good faith to align our ambitions with those of our organizations and the people we serve.

The Altruism of Ambition

If humankind is drawn to mountains, we are even more drawn to money. We work, we strive, we push ourselves. We want to succeed and we want to be rewarded monetarily for our success. Money drives us onward. It makes us creative. It forces us to be productive. And good things come from our pursuit of it! Entrepreneurs start businesses. Those businesses employ people. Those people innovate and create value for customers. As a society, we advance. A lot of good happens because someone had an idea for making money and had the ambition to pursue it.

The altruism of ambition is the idea that, paradoxically, being

selfish is way of being selfless. The economist John Maynard
Keynes once defined capitalism as "the astounding belief that
the most wickedest of men will do the most wickedest of things
for the greatest good of everyone." Although Keynes's definition
was tongue in cheek, it is not far off the mark. When people ambi-
tiously pursue their own self-interest, they often end up doing
great good for the community. That is how capitalism works. This
was Adam Smith's original and profound insight 250 years ago.
"It is not from the benevolence of the butcher, the brewer, or
the baker that we expect our dinner," he wrote "but from their
regard to their own interest."[2] By pursuing their own interests of
making money, they serve the greater good—making food and
drink available to those who want to buy them.

No system ever devised has been as effective at turning scar-
city into abundance as the one in which people are rewarded for
pursuing their own economic interest. Capitalism capitalizes on
people's inbuilt desire to be rewarded for their effort. It creates
opportunity like no other system in the world. Without intending to do so, personal ambition creates public benefits. Today we
have personal computers, lifesaving drugs, iPhones, fuel-efficient
cars. Which of these would have been invented if capitalistic
entrepreneurs had not perceived the rewards available to them
for bringing innovations to the market? Where would we be without self-interest, without ambition for more?

However, this perspective has diminishing returns at the
extremes. It is one thing to say that ambition creates opportunities or that self-interest is justifiable. It is another to say that
greed is good. Actor Michael Douglas won an Academy Award
in 1987 for playing Gordon Gecko, a fictitious financier, in the
film *Wall Street*. In the film's signature scene, Gecko addresses a

shareholder meeting of a company he plans to buy. Some of the shareholders are nervous about what Gecko will do to the company if he gains control. They fear he will be a greedy, merciless leader, willing to strip the company if he could make a buck for himself. In his speech, Gecko addresses their concerns head-on and explains that it is precisely because he will be greedy and merciless that he is the right person to buy the company. The scene is a large auditorium. The audience sits in rapt and silent attention. Gecko takes the microphone: "The point is that *greed,* for lack of a better word, is good. Greed is right, greed works. Greed clarifies, cuts through, and captures the essence of the evolutionary spirit. Greed, in all of its forms; greed for life, for money, for love, knowledge, has marked the upward surge of mankind."[3] In Gecko's world, greed is the genesis of all goodness. It is not prohibited. It is not merely permissible. It is a panacea. For Gordon Gecko, greed was more than good. It was God.

Gecko's character was outlandish, but he was compelling because he represented a truth. Our culture has grown more and more accustomed to the idea that businesspeople need only think of themselves and fulfilling their own ambition. "Since the time of Aristotle, and perhaps before," says philosopher Michael Novak, "business has been disparaged by people of culture and refinement. The critics of business have argued that the people who engage in it are selfish in their motivation, narrow in their interests, and instrumental in their behavior. In the last twenty years or so, something very odd has happened. This unattractive characterization of business, previously put forward only by those who were hostile to it, has been enthusiastically adopted by businesspeople themselves."

The Amnesia of Ambition

The problem with ambition, so poignantly portrayed in the character of Gordon Gecko, is that one can get carried away with it. A manager can become so single-minded that he forgets everything but the object of his ambition. Bowen McCoy was working together with a group of climbers to cross a moutain pass. By leaving them, he advanced his own ambitions, but he put his companions, not to mention the stranger, at risk.

Of course, managers are not the only ones susceptible to the amnesia of ambition; *anyone*, even aspiring pastors, can succumb. In 1973, John Darley and Daniel Batson published the results of a fascinating study they conducted at Princeton seminary.[4] The psychologists told a group of divinity students that they were conducting an experiment on how well the students were able to think on their feet by asking them to give extemporaneous speeches. Half the students were asked to give a talk on the parable of the Good Samaritan who stops and helps a poor stranger in need on the road. The other students were to talk about job opportunities postgraduation. The experimenters also divided the students into three groups. They told one-third of the students that they were late for the talk and needed to hurry. They told another third that they had just enough time and the last group that they had extra time.

Darley and Batson then asked the students to walk from one building to another to give their talk. In between the two buildings, they placed an actor who looked like a man in need of help, sunken on the ground directly in the path of the students as they went between buildings. As each student passed the actor, the man would groan and cough to show he was in trouble. The experimenters wanted to see which students would stop and help him.

They found that the topic of the students' talk had no bearing on whether the students stopped or not. The students who were speaking about the parable of the Samaritan helping the man on the side of the road were no more likely to help a flesh-and-blood person in need than were the students speaking about job opportunities. However, the experimenters did find a difference between the levels of helpfulness among the students. Those students who were told they had plenty of time were far more likely to help than those who were told they were running late. Those who were running late, regardless of the topic of their talk, walked around the man to get to their destination. In some cases, they stepped right over him. Like McCoy on the mountain, the students encountered a stranger in need of help. Those who, like McCoy, were under the pressure of time were apt to ignore the "problem" man and continue on their way.

Even in something as simple as an experiment in extemporaneous speaking, ambition can quickly devolve into blind ambition. By focusing so much on one goal, we can lose sight of everything else. And chances are, like the seminary students, we will not even realize it is happening. That is when it gets dangerous. That is when we may start making compromises that injure others, even our own companies, to get ahead ourselves. We begin to justify doing the unjustifiable. To put it differently, ambition can make us amnesiacs. In our single-minded search for self-advancement, we forget our duties to our organizations. We forget what we believe and what we value. We forget who we really are. We remember only the goal of our selfish ambition.

Bowen McCoy was later haunted by his decision on the

mountain. He never found out whether the sadhu lived and whether his own decision to push up the trail that day was justi-fied. He had brushed the "problem" aside and continued on his path. McCoy reflected on the encounter, "I had literally walked through a classic moral dilemma without thoughtfully thinking through the consequences. My excuses for my actions include a high adrenaline flow, a superordinate goal, and a once-in-a-lifetime opportunity—common factors in corporate situations, especially stressful ones."[5]

When someone makes an issue of a dilemma, it is easy to resent the inconvenience of having to deal with it rather than simply hiking onward. "Had we mountaineers been free of stress caused by the effort and the high altitude, we might have treated the sadhu differently," McCoy admits. "Yet isn't stress the real test of personal and corporate values? The instant decisions that executives make under pressure reveal the most about personal and corporate character. It is hard to predict when you will face moments of great stress and pressure. You can only predict that you will face them, and when you do, you will find what your real values are. Until those times come, your true motivations can remain hidden if you do not proactively address them.

Our capacity for rationalization and self-delusion is large. When money is on the line, it is even easier for our judgment to get clouded. One day in our negotiations class, the professor gave Max ten one-dollar bills. The professor told Max he had to offer some of the money to Amy, a classmate. If she accepted the offer, she would get whatever amount Max offered her and Max would get whatever amount remained. However, if she refused the offer, both would get nothing.

"Make the offer," said the professor.

Everyone's heads turned. Max thought about it for a moment. Amy looked across the room and smiled. Max took a moment more. Then Max made an MBA-like offer, "One dollar."

The smile vanished from Amy's face.

Amy's best alternative to *any* offer was to get nothing. Therefore, economic sense suggests she should accept any offer, including a lowball bid of one dollar because it would leave her better off than the alternative. Accepting the offer was the logical, profit-maximizing choice. Sure, she might be disappointed, but she would have to respect Max's supposedly keen business judgment and the inescapable power of economic logic.

Amy leaned forward on her desk. She looked straight at Max and said, "No."

The class erupted in applause, laughter, and high fives. Max, in his desire to maximize his own outcome, was blinded to how it would be perceived by other stakeholders. Although it seemed Amy was being irrational at first, her reaction actually made sense. One dollar to her was worth less than the joy of getting back at Max in retribution for him trying to take advantage of the situation. She eschewed the money. The applause and praise of her classmates was more than adequate compensation.

Max's experience fits squarely into the research of Kathleen Vohs, a professor at the University of Minnesota's Carlson School of Management. In 2008, she published an article describing the psychological consequences of introducing money into human interactions. Her conclusion? Money makes you mean. Vohs and her team used random samples of students and nonstudents at the University of Minnesota, Florida State University, and the University of British Columbia and divided their subjects into groups. The control group received neutral preconditioning while the "money prime" group was subtly reminded of money in various ways: by completing a word scramble puzzle that contained money references, looking at a poster depicting different currencies, moving stacks of play money or tokens, or reading an essay that mentioned money.

After the preconditioning, the groups were given a task or placed in a staged situation that tested measurable subconscious behavior. The subjects were asked for help by others in several scenarios: by the experimenter, by another participant, by a passerby who spilled a box of pencils in a random accident, or by the suggestion that they donate to the university student fund. It turns out the money-primed subjects offered to fill out fewer data sheets, spent less time helping a peer, picked up fewer pencils, and donated less to the student fund than did their neutral counterparts.[6] The students' minds had been altered by thinking about money. They forgot the standards of human decency they would have otherwise followed had they not had their minds on money and money on their minds.

Chicago public radio's *This American Life* once aired a show called "The Giant Pool of Money," which explained the global financial crisis and demonstrated how systemic greed can become.[7] The program profiled Mike Gardner, one of the loan brokers at Silver State Mortgage, the largest private mortgage bank in Nevada. The mortgage business, fueled by securitization, was growing quickly in the early 2000s. By 2003, most people who were qualified to get a mortgage already had one, so Mike had to find new borrowers if he was going to stay in business. That meant lending to people who never would have qualified for a loan before. In order to do that, he had to loosen the lending guidelines. His sales force, operating under commission, constantly reminded him that loosening the guidelines was the key to their success. Whenever they lost deals to someone else offering less-restrictive loan terms, they complained to Mike until he managed to get loan guidelines lowered again.

That is how the loan innovations began. "Three of [the sales guys] would show up at your door first thing in the morning and say, 'I lost ten deals last week to Bank Meritus. They've got this loan. Look at the guidelines for this loan. Is there any way we can do this?' I'd get on the phone and start calling all these street firms or Countrywide and say 'Would you buy this loan?' Finally, you'd find out who was buying them." Once Mike got a hit, he'd call back to the other firms and say he had a buyer for the loan, would they like to take the opportunity to buy too? "Once one person buys them, all the rest of them follow suit."[8]

It began with an innovation called a "stated income, verified asset loan," which meant a borrower did not have to provide paycheck stubs and W-2 forms, as they had in the past. They could simply *state* their income, as long as they proved that they had money in the bank. This brought in a lot of new business, so the brokers lowered the guideline restrictions again, and then again. Each time they loosened the restrictions, the loan business grew larger. They took in money hand over fist. The final innovation was the NINJA loan—no income, no job or asset verification. If you wanted a loan, you did not have to state a thing about how much money you made or what you possessed in assets. You just had to have a credit score. You could get a $500,000 loan even if you were unemployed and had no savings, as long as your credit was good.

Sound ridiculous and dangerous? It was, but not for Mike

Gardner's firm. They did not care how risky the mortgages were because they did not have to hold on to them for thirty years and see if they would be paid back, like they would have in the presecuritization days. The mortgage originator just owned the loans for a month or two and then sold them on to Wall Street as mortgage-backed securities. Wall Street banks would turn and trade them on as well, like a game of hot potato. The rest is history. All Mike cared about was whether his customers—the Wall Street investment banks—would buy those mortgages from him in the first place. Even at the time, Mike Gardner knew they were sowing the seeds of financial destruction. "My boss was in the business for twenty-five years. He hated those loans. He hated them and used to rant and say, 'It makes me sick to my stomach the kind of loans that we do.' He fought the owners and sales force tooth and neck about these guidelines."[9] Mike's boss always got the same reply: other firms are offering these loans so we will too. It's the only way to keep our share. Besides, home prices are skyrocketing. Everything will be fine. And it was, of course, until it wasn't. They were blinded by greed and by the naive assumption that if everyone else was offering the loans, they must be safe enough.

Why was everyone else doing it? At the end of the day, they did it because they could make a lot of money. As Dan and Chip Heath of *Fast Company* magazine put it, "When you're getting rich, it's pretty easy to soothe the ol' gut. If you need rationalization, your mind will provide one."[10] Self-interest had turned into greed and ambition had become blind. It happened across the system. Lenders like Silver State Mortgage pursued their self-interest, lowering loan restrictions so they could make ever-riskier loans and sell them on to securitizers. Each company and the individual managers within were thinking about their own bottom line, pursuing their own self-interest without regard for the broader risk. It was as if everyone was climbing the mountain in some kind of race, trying to reach the summit, willing to step on each other to get there. Then the mountain shook, an avalanche began; and everyone was brought down in a financial landslide of falling home prices, unpaid mortgages, and foreclosures.

The third promise of the MBA Oath is to not advance one's own narrow ambitions *at the expense of* one's enterprise and the people it serves. To advance oneself at the expense of one's firm is pure corruption. Lord Acton famously observed that "power tends to corrupt and absolute power corrupts absolutely." To this, David Young, the chairman of Oxford Analytica, adds, "It is important to understand the meaning of the word *corrupt* as much more than dishonest dealings. Rather, I believe Acton meant that the individual wielding the power loses his way, loses his bearings—behaves in a way he would not admit to or recognize in the cold light of day."[11] Young's comment squares with our understanding of ambition—it can blind you. We see it all the time.

Former Tyco CEO Dennis Kozlowski used the company's corporate treasury to pay for his personal living expenses and birthday parties. The Rigas family blended the Adelphia Company and family borrowings and guarantees for loans. Former New York Stock Exchange chairman Richard Grasso was suspected of too lightly regulating the listed firms that paid him a $150 million retirement package. Stock analyst Jack Grubman of Salomon Smith Barney changed his recommendation on AT&T stock after his boss asked him. It turns out that AT&T was also an investment banking client. In exchange, his parent company made a $1 million contribution to the kindergarten where Grubman was trying to get his daughter admitted. He was later fined $20 million and never allowed to work in the securities business again.

Examples of ambition blinding people and companies abound.

In each case, the individuals became like Bowen McCoy in the Himalayas, and like the seminarians at Princeton. We do not see the second-order consequences of looking out only for ourselves. We forget the implications of our actions. That is the problem of ambition. It gives us an acute economic amnesia. We forget everything but the object that drives us. So what do we do about it?

The Aspiration of Ambition

When we commit to manage our enterprises in good faith, it means we conduct our business with loyalty and care, both for the enterprise and for the people it serves. It means we can pursue our ambition but we have a commitment higher than our own ambition. It means drawing a distinction between self-interest and greed. Greed is not about having a desire for bad things. It is about having too strong a desire, an overzealous desire, for good things. Unbridled, greed pursues its goals to the exclusion and expense of others. That is, greed does not operate in a purely individual sense—it hurts other people as well.

We want to avoid two opposite, but equally possible, misunderstandings of the role of self-interest in capitalism, namely, that you should not pursue your self-interest at all or that you should think of greed as somehow good. We hold two beliefs in tension. First, we believe the pursuit of self-interest is vital to the engine of a capitalist economy. Second, despite the importance of pursuing one's self-interest, unbridled self-interest can unleash unbridled harm. These truths remain in tension, but the problem is not the tension between them. The problem arises when we ignore the tension and choose one truth to the exclusion of the other.

Trying to eliminate greed entirely is a fool's errand. In an article about the MBA Oath, a South African newspaper put it this way: "It's not that greed is good. It's that greed just *is*."[12] Perhaps the greatest strength of the American system of government is its realistic perspective of human nature. The founders of the republic were not naive idealists. They created a system of checks and balances because they recognized the selfish nature of humankind. On the other hand, the founders did assume other virtues would define the leaders of the republic and counterbalance the influence of greed. This is the driving point of the third promise of the MBA Oath. We cannot eliminate greed, but we can (and should) bridle it.

One way to begin bridling our greed and ambition is to reform the incentives baked in to current compensation policies. In order to align the interests of managers and shareholders, many companies now tie compensation packages for managers, even junior managers, to quarterly share prices. Yet we would argue that this actually encourages a short-term mindset of rapid personal enrichment. Shareholders should rightly be concerned about managers doing things that drive up the share price quickly at the expense of a firm's lasting health. The incentives for executives with stock options are skewed toward reckless risk taking. Heads they win, tails they break even. If managers are going to be greedy, they should be long-term greedy, and they should not be given perverse compensation schemes that incentivize them to roll the dice with their companies' futures.

Institutional reforms will be a long time coming, and may potentially create as many problems as they attempt to solve. In the meantime, managers must decide what principles will govern their decision making when times of trial arise. Bowen McCoy lacked a set of principles to guide his actions, and the unknown fate of the sadhu haunts him still. "One of our problems was that we as a group had no process for developing consensus," McCoy writes. "We had no sense of purpose or plan. The difficulties of dealing with the sadhu were so complex that no one person could handle them. Because the group did not have a set of preconditions that could guide its action to an acceptable resolution, we reacted instinctively as individuals."[13] The MBA Oath aims to supplement this natural instinct with an awareness of our duties as managers.

We have argued elsewhere in this book that managers should not overfocus on shareholder value to the extreme detriment of the firm's other stakeholders. The point of this pledge is that managers should not overfocus on their own ambition to the detriment of their shareholders. Managers have a duty to create shareholder value, and while enlightened self-interest can align our ambitions with those of their shareholders, we must pledge not to let our self-interest turn into greed.

The alternative to greed is good faith. It is to act as a fiduciary for your enterprise and the people it serves. As the Model Business Corporation Act puts it, "A corporate director or officer shall discharge his or her duties as a director or officer *in good faith,* with the care an ordinarily prudent person in a like position would exercise under similar circumstances; in a manner he reasonably believes to be in the best interests of the corporation."[14] Acting in good faith means you cannot engage in "self-dealing." For example, if an electronics store sells Peter a laptop for a price that is three standard deviations higher than the average retail price for that computer, he cannot rescind the contract or sue for damages. It was Peter's responsibility to find the better price. However, if a corporate officer sold sixty laptops to her company at such inflated prices, she would be crossing the fiduciary line. It is her responsibility to be fair. Her fiduciary obligations prohibit such self-dealing. Legendary judge Benjamin Cardozo, in his opinion for the case of *Meinhard v. Salmon,* summarizes the idea of fiduciary duty this way: "Joint adventurers, like copartners, owe to one another, while the enterprise continues, the duty of the finest loyalty. Many forms of conduct permissible in a workday world for those acting at arm's length, are forbidden to those bound by fiduciary ties. A trustee is held to something stricter than the morals of the market place. *Not honesty alone, but the punctilio of an honor the most sensitive, is then the standard of behavior.*"[15] There is a calling higher than our ambition, and that is our honor.

＝＝＝

We must be watchful and recognize the sadhu when he comes into our lives. The sadhu can take the form of an employee with a grave disease, a spouse sitting alone at home, a customer unable to pay the bill when due, or a shareholder expecting a return on capital invested. As we make our way up the mountain, focused obsessively on our own ambitions, we may leave some to die on the trail. Though we reach the summit, we shall ever after be plagued by the question, "What was the price of my success?" As professionals, we need to remember the rules of the mountain. It is more important for everyone to get down alive than for one person to reach the top.

9

THE LETTER AND THE
SPIRIT OF THE LAW

I will understand and uphold, both in letter and in spirit,
the laws and contracts governing my own conduct and that
of my enterprise. If I find laws that are unjust, antiquated, or
unhelpful I will not brazenly break, ignore, or avoid them; I
will seek civil and acceptable means of reforming them.

MBA Oath, Fourth Promise

Through the MBA Oath, I look forward to standing up with
my peers and joining in the promise to hold myself to a
higher standard of behavior and conduct and to working
for the greater good of society. We must remember "from
everyone who has been given much, much will be required."

Teal Carlock, Harvard Business School,
Class of 2009, signer #8

A gas station owner in Ohio worries that he may be forced
to shut down his gas station because a newly enacted
state law requires gas stations to pump gas with at least
10 percent ethanol. He is concerned that he cannot find the
$200,000 he will need in order to replace decades-old storage
tanks with newer double-lined tanks utilized for ethanol-added

fuel. Following the law would mean incurring a financial burden that could end his livelihood.

A close friend and classmate spent numerous hours negotiating a contract with a third-party data provider of industry information, similar to Bloomberg or Thomson. It was her first job out of business school and she wanted to make her mark—to show that she could get things done. The contract was expensive and she was negotiating complex terms on behalf of her ten-person department. Following the close of the contract agreement, a senior vice president from a different department approached her for access to the industry information. The problem was that giving this vice president access would violate the contractual agreement with the data provider. She grappled with following the terms of the contract at the expense of alienating her coworkers and her own stature at her new job.

The fourth promise of the MBA Oath is to respect and abide by the law and the contracts that bind you, both in letter and in spirit. What do we mean by this? In essence, we mean treating the written law as a minimum duty to guide our actions. Instead of referring to the law as a maximum code of conduct, under which all other unarticulated activities are allowed, we view the law as a minimum hurdle for conduct. In this chapter we look at the law as an impediment to business, the law as an enabler of business, and why we ought to uphold the letter and the spirit of the law.

The Law as an Impediment to Business

Many see the law and regulation as an impediment to good and efficient business practices. They view the law as an instrument of coercion and constraint that ultimately reduces productivity and diminishes profits. Take the owner of the gas station in Ohio mentioned earlier. The gas station owner's lament is that a regulation aimed at reducing the United States' dependence on foreign oil has created a set of unintended consequences. Namely, he incurs a large input cost to achieve the same output.

The same lament is heard in many sectors of business, whether it be the financial sector, health care, manufacturing, or nearly any other sector of our economy. Government laws and regulations purportedly increase costs, slow down decision-making processes, and restrict access to resources necessary to provide essential goods to the marketplace. Such regulations, many argue, engender a bloated bureaucracy that seeks to overregulate in its zeal to justify its own existence. Businesses are forced to fill out additional paperwork, incur expenses of hiring compliance officers, pay for attorneys to interpret regulations, wait in endless lines, make countless telephone calls, seek multiple kinds of permits, or participate in compliance and review hearings, all of which increases the cost of doing business.

Sarbanes-Oxley may be an example of regulatory overreach. The law was intended to prevent such scandals as those that brought down Enron and WorldCom. A 2008 Securities and Exchange Commission survey of officers at publicly traded firms concluded that Sarbanes-Oxley cost the average company $2.3 million a year in direct compliance costs. For many small businesses, that is a staggeringly high number and is an example of the cost of a regulatory scheme potentially outweighing the benefit derived from such a scheme.

And what about innovation? Many business entrepreneurs view regulation and the law as a wrench clogging the machinery of business. They argue that regulation stifles creativity and innovation. It stymies new technologies. Medicines to treat and cure diseases may be available elsewhere in the world, but they are unavailable in the United States because of regulatory impasses created by the federal Food and Drug Administration. The antiregulation lobby argues that overregulation may indeed be costing lives or standing in the way of individuals enjoying a quality life.

Antiregulation sentiments are most often expressed by those who value individual freedom as the primary moral principle in our society. Under that view, the most important duty of government is to assure that the state offers maximal protection to the concept of individual freedom and choice. Under this view, individuals should be free of governmental interference with their lives, their choices, or the use of their property. Special interests abound, and the prospect of governmental regulators increasing their personal power through expansive application of rules is a greater threat than any threat the regulators are supposedly reducing in the interest of the "common good."

The Law as Enabler of Business

The opposite view is that the law does not inhibit business; it enables business. The law has advanced the needs of business and brought about prosperity and happiness in the greater social order. In the first instance, the law is what makes business possible in the first place. Corporations and other forms of business exist by virtue of the consent of the people acting through their legislators. The law provides certainty and finality in business dealings. Without the law, contracts would not be binding or enforceable. The law creates trust and encourages the establishment of trust relationships (and in some instances, fiduciary relationships).

This trust and certainty from well-established business law accrue in tangible ways to businesspeople. As we have mentioned earlier in the book, transaction costs diminish in societies where business law is well developed and enforceable. Costs of capital—the cost to borrow money—are dramatically reduced as lenders feel a greater sense of certainty over their own recourse should default occur. The strength of a country's laws and institutions go a long way in explaining a country's economic performance. Consider the number of days it takes to get a license for starting a new business in the United States versus other countries. In the United States, it takes 5 days. In Paraguay, 74. In Laos, 198.[1] Entrepreneurship is hard enough as it is; it becomes much harder if you have to wait two thirds of a year to get started. Moreover, in many societies property rights are not upheld and protected. Some governments expropriate the earnings and assets of thriving businesses, substantially reducing incentives for hard work and entrepreneurship.

The enforcement mechanisms of the law provide for consequences in the event of a breach of trust relationships or other contract promises. The law serves to protect expectations, including expectations of profits and opportunities. To the extent anyone complains about the "interference" of the law in business dealings, the plain fact is business dealings would be all but impossible without the law.

To the extent that the law imposes standards and sets certain minimum requirements in the production of goods and services, the interests of business are served and expenses can be reduced. For example, by having national standards regarding freight and the conduct of freight movement either on highways or by rail, business managers have the assurance that freight will be handled pursuant to certain common standards regardless of what state it is shipped from or to and regardless of local customs or parochial interests.

The law makes it possible to seek justice when a company does business in one's home state and then seeks to avoid the obligations of a business deal by claiming the company hails from another state and is beyond the court's jurisdiction. This protects business expectations and interests and in the long run saves a great deal of money. Though seemingly onerous at times, the disclosure requirements of the Securities and Exchange Commission make it possible to have a much fuller understanding of a business investment than simply trusting a fellow's word that "this is a good deal." Regulation of these sales insures and protects investors and promotes the overall health of the economy.

In what has been hailed as the "most comprehensive cost/benefit study conducted on government regulations," the Office of Management and Budget (OMB) during the George W. Bush administration concluded that most regulations in fact have a major positive impact on the environment and public health.[2] "EPA regulations limiting emissions from engines used for recreational, nonroad purposes cost $192 million per year to comply with, but they save the operators more than twice that—$410 million per year—in lower operating costs. Additionally, there are even bigger savings in health and environmental protection, estimated between $900 million and $7.88 billion in air quality benefits this year! And this does not even include some benefits that the OMB recognized but was unable to quantify, such as reductions in infant mortality from the cleaner air."[3]

Commentator John Marty, writing on the subject, commented further, "the health and social benefits of enforcing tough new clean-air regulations during the past decade were *five to seven times greater* in economic terms than were the costs of complying with the rules. The value of reductions in hospitalization and emergency room visits, premature deaths, and lost workdays resulting from improved air quality were estimated between $120 billion and $193 billion from October 1992 to September 2002. By comparison, industry, states and municipalities spent an estimated $23 billion to $26 billion to retrofit plants and facilities and make other changes to comply with new clean-air standards."[4] The challenge is that the costs of these regulations are borne by specific firms while the benefits accrue to everyone. So for an individual firm, the cost of compliance with a good law can still be greater than the benefit.

The Spirit of the Law

Which view is right? Is the law an inhibitor or an enabler of business? We take a middle view—the law can both inhibit or enable business. On one hand, the law protects property, enforces contracts, and creates a culture of trust. On the other hand, it can create a culture of distrust and litigiousness; and regulation can lead to its own moral hazard. The MBA Oath is a commitment to uphold the laws and contracts when they are just, seek to reform them when they are unjust, and respect them always. The MBA Oath is intended to stir dialogue about the commitment of business leaders to the community as a whole, to be concerned about the public good, and, in the process, to advance and defend as necessary the dictates of the law toward meeting those ends.

A recent law school graduate was puzzled by the pledge in the MBA Oath to uphold the law. He argued that the fear of punishment at the hands of the law should be sufficient, and a pledge to uphold the law was all but irrelevant. When punishment alone is advanced as the reason for following the law, the legal system turns into another game where the object is to bluff the system and reap the reward. In such a system, the only benefit of following the law is avoiding punishment. So, if someone finds a way to break the law or to just "bend it a little" without getting caught, inveterate game theorists might find the concept at worst amoral and at best "a win." The law is not valued for its own sake, but viewed only as an impediment to be overcome like any other business obstacle.

Another problem arising from a strictly "legalistic" response to corporate misbehavior is that the law will be perceived as setting the highest standards one must adhere to in order to act ethically in business decisions. Former secretary of state James Baker once said, "Ever more complex regulation sometimes encourages ethical corner-cutting by suggesting that just legalistic compliance is sufficient. That is what we might call the moral hazard of over-regulation."[5] Thus the regulation, though intended to define "minimal standards" of acceptable behavior, is interpreted by actors in the marketplace as the highest standard required of a business.

The law should not be viewed as setting "maximum" requirements for ethical business conduct. In fact, many of the law's regulatory requirements are deemed to be "minimum" standards for compliance. For example, federal safety standards regarding motor vehicles are set forth in regulations written in terms of "minimum safety performance requirements" for motor vehicles or items of motor vehicle equipment. The Consumer-Patient Radiation Health and Safety Act directs the secretary of Health and Human Services to develop "minimum" standards for state certification and licensure of persons who administer ionizing or nonionizing radiation in the fields of medicine and dentistry.

Developing standards is important for public health, but many federal and state regulations suggest only "minimum" standards. Yet businesspeople tend to think of them in terms of the "maximum" standard they must achieve in order to meet their professional obligations. The law recognizes that a "reasonable standard" of care may be imposed on a person or a company in producing a product or marketing a product. This "reasonable standard" is ultimately defined by a jury, and businesses should be wary of believing that a jury will always conclude that a "reasonable" standard of care is coincident with "minimum" standards established by state or federal agencies in any given enterprise. Juries may well impose a higher standard, believing a higher standard is the more reasonable standard to be upheld.

Following the damage caused by the global financial crisis, many people screamed, "There ought to be a law" or "Why wasn't that conduct illegal?" In some instances, the conduct complained of was illegal. In other instances, it was legal—for example, the provision of loans to potentially uneducated borrowers—but the public outcry suggests that legislators or regulators should consider passage of laws or regulations that prevent such behavior in the future. The tectonic plates of Wall Street collide with the tectonic plates of Main Street. Should new regulation—such as limits on loans to subprime borrowers and minimum capital requirements for banks—be enacted? At this juncture, that question has largely already been answered. With a high degree of certainty, new laws will be created. The important message is that because businesspeople did not take into account any higher calling than what they could get away with—that is, they did not consider the spirit of the law—they will suffer through a new set of regulations that could be similarly taxing as that of Sarbanes-Oxley.

Drugs and Hybrids: Law, Society, and Business

What if you had the opportunity to deliver the world's top AIDS medication to some of the world's poorest people for less than a sixth of the prevailing price? You might think you had the chance to win the Nobel Peace Prize. But what if doing so violated the patents of other pharmaceutical firms and put your home country at risk of losing its membership in the World Trade Organization (WTO)? What does it look like to uphold the letter and spirit of the law in this case?

In 2003, Cipla was the third largest drug company in India. It had made a fortune by reverse engineering expensive patented drugs and selling them at low prices (a strategic necessity for a country whose per-person average income was only $350 per year). At the time, India's patent laws recognized patents protecting the process of making a product but were not protective of the product itself. Thus, Cipla's reverse-engineering strategy was well within the permissive legal boundaries of the society. Even Mahatma Gandhi had endorsed the company.

India, however, was poised to join the World Trade Organization. Membership in the WTO required India to recognize and respect twenty-year product patents on pharmaceuticals and other products developed around the world. Though Cipla's business model was well within national legal standards and societal norms, it violated the international convention. Cipla's business model was in trouble.

The CEO of Cipla, Dr. Yusuf Hamied, fiercely defended his company. He framed the dilemma this way: "I think the multinationals made a big mistake pricing [AIDS medicines] at $12,000 to $15,000 for something that costs them $200. Today, only 30,000 people in the whole of Africa are being treated; 9,000 are dying

each day [because affordable medicines are not available] . . .
I am accused of having an ulterior motive. *Of course* I have an
ulterior motive: before I die, I want to do some good."[6]

Others in the pharmaceutical industry did not view Cipla's
actions so altruistically. J. P. Garnier, the CEO of drug giant
GlaxoSmithKline, said of Cipla, "They're pirates. That's about
what they are . . . they've never done a day of research in their
lives."[7] Garnier's criticism was not without basis in fact. He and
other members of the pharmaceutical industry refused to yield
the moral high ground to Hamied and Cipla. Only a handful of
nations in the world develop new drugs because only a handful
of nations employ strict patent laws to protect and incentivize
innovators. The reason pharmaceutical businesses are among the
most profitable in the world is that patents are utilized to protect
new drugs. Patents in turn serve as a huge monetary incentive
to the development of new drugs and medicines. Research and
development costs range in the billions of dollars. In order for a
pharmaceutical company to take on that risk, it has to be assured
of a payoff. The payoff comes in the form of a protected stream of
revenue derived from a short-term monopoly backed by the legal
standard of patents.

Is this an instance where the spirit of the law—saving people's
lives—is of higher value than the current letter of patent laws protecting business profits? We are not implying that and it would be
irresponsible of us to do so in such a flippant manner. However,
it does surface the idea of how, on occasion, the law may not provide a manager with the clarity to operate. That is where the oath
comes in and acknowledges the importance of law, the spirit of
the law, and other factors such as sustainable prosperity. Though
the company defends its behavior on humanitarian grounds, the
long-term trade-off is that the incentive to create new drugs to

fight emerging diseases and maladies is commensurately weakened, and those countries which spend the time and effort to develop remedies for human illness are made to carry the burden of those that do not engage in such humanitarian efforts.

Consider a different case. Does it make a difference if the issue is premised on the reverse engineering of Viagra instead of AIDs treatment drugs? Though this may give rise to "human" concerns, it does not invite a response based upon "humanitarian" concerns. What about clean energy or hybrid cars? Until the recall of the Prius in early 2010, the Toyota hybrid was the auto industry's gold standard for balancing social, environmental, and economic considerations. In 2009 the *Wall Street Journal* reported that Toyota was building a thicket of patents around its hybrid technology to block competition and preserve its market power. The Toyota case exemplifies the trade-offs we face in creating economic, social, and environmental value. Although granting Toyota the patents may impair the social value of placing more hybrids on the road, Toyota is not without justification in claiming monetary compensation for its ingenuity. Where lies the balance between global social norms and the law? Is the purpose of the law to inspire and incentivize innovation and discovery for the long-term or to address immediate ripening concerns in health or the environment? One economist put the problem this way: On the one hand, "protecting intellectual property preserves market power, and thus destroys social value." On the other hand, "innovation creates social value and unless we allow inventors to capture some of this value, there is little incentive to create value."[8]

We do not pretend that making decisions about "social value" is easy or that we have it all figured out. Our intention is not so much to lay out rules for managers to follow as much as it is to get managers to be more thoughtful about these decisions. These economic versus social value trade-offs *already* exist. Our hope is that the MBA Oath will be a reminder to managers to think about the trade-offs carefully and plan accordingly. They do not always have to choose one side over the other, but they should always make decisions with a profound sense that they are affecting a broader group of stakeholders than their shareholders and fellow managers.

To be more precise in the context of our discussion, when there are great moral, ethical, and business goods at stake, there is an integrating and prioritizing that must occur. We must balance the lesser goods, such as the next quarterly earnings report, with the greater goods, such as fulfilling our business mission and contributing to society.

We encourage business managers to think in terms of "first things," to approach their decisions from the standpoint of a much larger picture. Ronald Heifetz, leadership professor at Harvard's Kennedy School of Government, says that leaders need to "get on the balcony" to achieve a rightful perspective. We know this is hard to do when you are a beginning or middle-level manager down in the arena and sand is being thrown in your face. Still, as Heifetz says, "Stand on the balcony." Get the long view. Where will you be ten years from now as you reflect back on the decision you made today? If you place "second things first," will you make a compromise that ultimately costs much more? It is no more than a moral Ponzi scheme, and eventually, you may discover that your trade-offs with the law or your own inner moral guide will catch up with you. Standing on the balcony means moving beyond the next quarter's report and considering the legacy you leave not only to your stockholders and employees but also to future generations.

Your legacy is ensured when you show respect for the law, meaning you work within the boundaries of the law but then challenge and seek change in the law when justice, mercy, and normative moral obligations demand a courageous and sustained effort to bring the law into compliance with doing what is simply the right thing to do.

RESPONSIBILITY AND TRANSPARENCY

I will take responsibility for my actions, and I will represent the performance and risks of my enterprise accurately and honestly.

MBA Oath, Fifth Promise

A firm's income statement may be likened to a bikini—what it reveals is interesting, but what it conceals is vital.

Economist Burton G. Malkiel

We can create value for society by conducting business with strong ethics. My hope is that this will become the norm rather than the exception. And at precisely this point, our oath will seem redundant rather than peculiar.

Jimmy Tran, Harvard, Class of 2009, signer #7

Peter Andersen had been the CEO of Beech-Nut for only a year when it happened. The Nestlé-owned subsidiary was a maker of baby food, the last place on earth one would expect this kind of intrigue to occur. Andersen's first year had been a success. He had been charged with turning the company around and by all accounts he was off to a good start. His secret weapon: apple juice. The big push was to focus Beech-Nut's marketing on the nutritional value of its products, especially the juices. Nutrition was becoming a major trend in baby food in the early 1980s as consumers increased their nutritional knowledge and began to prefer natural products in growing numbers. Under Andersen's direction, each baby-focused bottle of juice was labeled "100% fruit juice" and "No Sugar Added." With the changes, juice sales skyrocketed by almost 70 percent from the previous year, leading to a company turnaround. At the time of the incident, apple juice alone accounted for 30 percent of Beech-Nut's total sales. The young CEO never expected that the product he thought would save the company might eventually lead to his own undoing.[1]

As Peter Andersen entered the office on June 28, 1982, his vice president of finance gave him distressing news. A private investigator had visited one of Beech-Nut's plants early that morning. The investigator claimed to represent PAI, the Processed Apples Institute. He informed the plant manager that one of Beech-Nut's suppliers was substituting sugar water for apple juice concentrate. He wanted Beech-Nut to join a class-action lawsuit against the supplier.

For five years, Universal Juice Company had been Beech-Nut's single biggest juice supplier. Universal claimed they imported Israeli apples and blended the concentrate at a plant in Queens, New York. Despite the exotic source of their ingredients, Universal's price continued to be 20 to 25 percent cheaper than any other supplier. Universal's juice worked well for Beech-Nut. The previous year Beech-Nut's juice (made from Universal concentrate) was ranked the best juice on the market by the *New York Times,* and the only juice out of thirteen tested to be called "100% juice."

Still, the private investigator's theatrical early morning visit raised alarms in Andersen's mind. A few years earlier, Beech-Nut had concerns about the quality of Universal's concentrate and had sent two employees to review Universal's mixing process. Oddly, instead of seeing mixing tanks and pumps, they found only an empty warehouse. As a result, Beech-Nut forced Universal to sign an agreement saying Universal would be liable if the juice was found to be adulterated. A year later, one test found the Universal concentrate to be pure sugar syrup, but Beech-Nut failed to act upon this information. Subsequent tests failed to detect such problems. Beech-Nut stayed with Universal and continued to receive a steady 20 percent reduction in supply costs.

If Andersen were required to switch suppliers, he would kill the margins on his biggest selling product. If that happened, the company would go into the red, and Nestlé might be required to close down the division or sell it. Andersen's job was on the line. His production manager said there was no conclusive way to test for juice purity without knowing exactly which additives might have been used, but the PAI detective said the institute had a private test not yet adopted by the FDA that was conclusive. Should Beech-Nut pursue the test? Should they tell Nestlé of the risk? Andersen did not know what to do, nor did he realize that the private investigator's visit would launch one of the most fateful decisions of his career.

The Importance of Being Honest

The fifth promise of the MBA Oath is to take responsibility for your actions and to be honest about the performance and risks of your enterprise. Responsibility means that when things go badly, my reaction will not be to blame others but to own the outcome myself. It means that if the numbers do not look good on paper, I will not fudge them, I will be transparent; and I will explain them.

As with some of the other principles of the MBA oath, the fifth pledge is one that seems so obvious that it might be overlooked. Yet this simple principle is so important that it could almost stand alone as an oath pledge without regard to the other oath promises. Just consider what your life would be like and what your performance would be like if you always took responsibility for your actions, honored your promises and represented yourself accurately and honestly. Instead of your life being filled with cracks, fissures, and fragmentation, you would walk with solid and even terrain beneath your feet. Your life would be built upon a rock, not shifting sands.

Economist Michael Jensen has gone so far as to argue that honoring one's word is a *"fundamental"* requirement for business success. The benefits of honoring your word are much greater than the costs of not doing so. Remember that integrity means not simply "acting ethically" but also "the quality or state of being complete, unbroken, or whole." Taking responsibility for one's actions goes to the heart of acting with integrity. Jensen explains the concept with the example of dealing with an object that might not have integrity—your car. "When it is not whole and complete and unbroken (that is a component is missing or malfunctioning), it becomes unreliable, unpredictable, and it creates those characteristics in our lives. The car fails in traffic, we create a traffic jam, we are late for appointments, fail to perform, disappoint our partners, associates, and firms. In effect, the out-of-integrity car creates a lack of integrity in our life. . . ."[2] It is like the old poem describing the fall of Richard III:

For want of a nail the shoe was lost.
For want of a shoe the horse was lost.
For want of a horse the rider was lost.
For want of a rider the battle was lost.
For want of a battle the kingdom was lost.
And all for the want of a horseshoe nail.

When one piece is broken, it impairs everything else in our life. Jensen contends that what is true of cars is also true of people and organizations. If a person cannot be trusted to honor their commitments and duties, that person can cause chaos throughout the organization. The integrity of organizations depends on people, and the integrity of people depends on them taking responsibility for their actions. One person's failure to keep his or her word can create a crack in business relationships that can severely frustrate the successful and smooth operation of the business.

Transparency and trust are critical not only for individuals, but also for organizations and entire societies. Unless investors can trust the numbers, they will not provide the capital necessary to fuel the company's growth. If companies are unable or unwilling to abide by their promises, the network of business relationships upon which the economy depends is fractured, and the economy suffers. Trust is essential to the health of an economy. After the economic crisis, banks are wary and distrustful of individuals and businesses seeking loans. The failure of companies to keep their promises to pay their obligations on time has fractured those relationships. Trade has suffered, and the economy has teetered on the brink of collapse. A credit crunch is in essence a trust issue, an issue arising from broken promises and the refusal of people to take responsibility for their own actions.

In the real world, of course, it is impossible to always keep your promises, and this can lead to an erosion of trust. However, as Jensen surprisingly points out, it is still possible to *honor* your word, even when you cannot *keep* your word. One way to honor your word is to keep the promise as made. The second way in which you may honor your word is when you understand that you will not be able to keep a promise, you announce that fact to everyone impacted and accept responsibility for the impact of your decisions on others. In this way, Jensen explains, you still have integrity because you "maintain your word as whole and complete."[3]

According to a recent study of service businesses, 23.3 percent of "memorable satisfactory encounters involve difficulties attributable to failures in core service delivery."[4] Almost one-quarter of the experiences of satisfied customers arose from a circumstance where a company failed to provide the service! Nevertheless, the customers apparently were satisfied with the integrity of the company and the manner in which the failures were explained or compensated. Sometimes simply saying, "I am sorry for my mistake" is all that may be necessary to heal a broken promise. We have experienced this phenomenon firsthand.

Max switched to a new cell phone carrier a couple of years ago. One day his text messages stopped working. He could receive them, but was not able to send. He felt steamed about this and called the customer service line. When he told the customer representative about the problem, the representative said, "Sir, that sounds frustrating. I know if I were in your shoes, I would be disappointed. Text messages are an important part of your plan. Let me apologize for the mistake, get it fixed for you, and credit your account for the inconvenience." When Max called, he was prepared to give a piece of his mind, but the customer service person's reply was so disarmingly honest and responsible, it diffused the frustration. The company was transparent about the error and took responsibility to rectify the situation. Max's faith in the company was quickly restored.

East of Eden

Peter Andersen failed to comprehend the importance of accepting personal accountability for his own actions. A few days after the encounter with the private investigator, Andersen chose to ignore the investigator's accusations. He concerned himself instead with the day-to-day business of improving the company's profit and loss statement at year's end. No internal investigations occurred. It was a mistake.

About a month later, FDA inspectors paid a surprise visit to the Beech-Nut plant. They collected samples of apple juice for further testing. Then, a few days later, the New York State Department of Agriculture and Markets informed Beech-Nut that they had tested a sample of the company's apple juice purchased from a retail store and found it had been adulterated.

With the questions looming, what would you do as CEO? Stop production? Pull products off the shelf? Do nothing? Andersen went to the bunker vehemently arguing the tests were inconclusive. Beech-Nut's concentrate was imported, he argued, suggesting that Israeli apples might have different chemical properties.

The state threatened to seize Beech-Nut's juice inventory. Losing the juice would cost the company five dollars a case. Andersen refused to accept such a consequence and instead considered the option of shipping his juice inventory out of New York. Once out of New York, state authorities would have no jurisdiction to seize it. He consulted the company's lawyers. They said the transfer was technically legal. So Andersen ordered thirty thousand cases of apple juice transferred out of state to a warehouse in Secaucus, New Jersey.

Andersen's actions might have delayed consequences, but they did not avoid them. Even as the eighteen-wheelers rolled into the Garden State (we imagine the radios in their cabs blaring Springsteen's "Born to Run"), Andersen learned that the U.S. Food and Drug Administration was considering seizing the inventory. They too had concluded the apple juice samples were adulterated.

Now what would you do as CEO? Turn your products over? Issue a public apology to worried parents? Again, Andersen chose to avoid consequences and ordered the inventory moved once again, this time by selling off a third of the inventory and then shipping the remaining twenty thousand cases of concentrate to distributors in Puerto Rico and the Dominican Republic (beyond FDA jurisdiction) at discounts of up to 50 percent.

Andersen's refusal to take responsibility for his actions resulted in a federal indictment of both Andersen and the company on charges of adulterated and misbranded products. Three days before the trial was to begin, Beech-Nut pleaded guilty to 215 felony counts of adulteration. Beech-Nut was hit with a $2 million fine, the largest ever at that time. They also paid out $7.5 million in a class-action civil suit. Andersen himself was sentenced to five years' probation and a massive personal fine.

Business Bluffing: Shirking Responsibility

The Beech-Nut case was not the first, nor will it be the last, of an executive seeking to avoid consequences, both personal and corporate, by turning a blind eye to the truth. The McKesson and Robbins scandal of the late 1930s involved the use of forged warehouse receipts as collateral for loans. In the 1960s, Billie Sol Estes of Texas falsified the number of fertilizer tanks he had under lease and borrowed against the fictitious larger number. Anthony "Tino" De Angelis hoodwinked American Express by using tanks of "salad oil" as collateral for loans. Of course, we know that oil is less dense than water, but only Tino knew that he had floated a six-inch layer of salad oil on top of twenty feet of water to secure those loans.[5]

Such shenanigans are not infrequent. The question is why people believe they can get away with their tricks and deceits. How can a man as intelligent and successful as Peter Andersen convince himself that his schemes could be hidden? Are businesspersons so used to playing "bluffing" games in negotiations and business deals that the bluff becomes a practice and pattern of business—even when the subjects of the bluff are state and federal authorities?

A friend of ours works for a television production company and negotiates deals with cable and satellite firms to carry his company's content. He states that the way deals get done in his business is dependent upon good bluffing. "If I'm totally transparent with exactly what our company would agree to, we'd get eaten alive in negotiations," he says. "When we go into a negotiation, I'm not going to tell the other side what we'd settle for the moment I walk into a room, and I know they're not going to tell me either. That's how the game is played." Our friend's use of the word "game" was telling, and was a very good point. Most business negotiations are indeed approached like a game, where all the players understand it would be unwise to reveal their strategies too early.

In 1968, Albert Z. Carr wrote a classic article called "Is Business Bluffing Ethical?" Carr argued that businesspeople ought to think of business as a game, specifically, the game of poker. "In poker it is right and proper to bluff a friend out of the rewards of being dealt a good hand. A player feels no more than the slightest twinge of sympathy if—when with nothing better than a single ace in his hand—he strips another player of the remainder of his chips, even though the other player may in fact have a better hand. It was up to the other fellow to protect himself. In the words of an excellent poker player, former president Harry Truman, 'If you can't stand the heat, stay out of the kitchen.' "[6] Carr says that no one thinks less of poker because its rules are different from the rules governing the rest of human behavior. In the same way, he proceeds, no one should think less of the game of business if its standards of right and wrong do not match those of the rest of society. In the game of business, bluffing is allowed, even expected, and therefore it is permissible. Falsehood, said British statesman Henry Taylor, ceases to be falsehood when it is understood on all sides that the truth is not expected to be spoken. Why limit one's ability to take advantage of opportunities that are permitted by the rules of the game?

Even though the game of poker allows bluffing, poker is not without ethical rules. "The man who keeps an ace up his sleeve or who marks the cards is more than unethical;" Carr writes, "he is a crook, and can be punished as such—kicked out of the game or, in the Old West, shot."[7] In the same way, there are limits to bluffing in business. In a negotiation, you do not have to tell your counterparty your reservation price, but neither should you lie about qualities of your product or service so as to fraudulently induce them to enter a contract. It may seem a subtle distinction, but it is a distinction. Many people miss it and assume that if bluffing is permitted, then there must be other permissible ways to misrepresent the truth. This may have been what happened to Peter Andersen. The lines between bluffing and lying became blurred, and he lost track of where one ended and the other began.

A second possible reason for Andersen's failure was his fear of failure itself. The more one is afraid of failure, the more one becomes willing to compromise in order to avoid failure. Michael Jensen offers a helpful framework to understand this issue, the "Integrity-Performance Paradox." When people and organizations are systematically committed to performance, they often sacrifice integrity in the name of increasing performance; but in doing so, they ultimately end up reducing performance. As with the Beech-Nut case, so it is with bluffing; though it may seemingly pay to sacrifice honesty in the short-term (why else would one do it?), in the long-term, such decisions often return to haunt the decision makers. Enron is a classic example.

Enron was once the seventh largest company in the United States, worth $62.5 billion at the beginning of 2001. One year later, its stock was worth only pennies. The company's collapse left thousands of employees without jobs, and millions of pensioners and investors with huge losses. It was the largest bankruptcy in American history. During the good times, the senior managers at Enron received incentives by selling the stock options they had received from the company. Thus, they had a significant personal interest in seeing earnings rise. The faster Enron's profits grew, the higher the price of Enron stock went; the more valuable the stock options, the wealthier the owners of the options became.[8] Senior leaders of the company were so obsessed with growth that they sacrificed their integrity for stock performance utilizing a variety of accounting techniques to cloak expenses, real revenue streams, and the bottom-line value of the company.

In the meantime, Enron's board of directors was rated as one of the "top five in the United States for its overall corporate governance structure and guidelines." But the board completely failed to police the internal management of the company. Enron's so-called independent audits consisted of "culturization" of the work teams, where various auditors were encouraged to work together on the same floor as the people they were auditing, implicitly developing personal alliances with one another. Enron's auditors were paid $2 million a year for their watchdog audit services at the same time they were being paid $25 million a year for "consulting" services.[9] Think about that. If the auditors receive $2 million a year to scrutinize books and act as watchdogs, and at the same time they receive $25 million a year for consulting, where will their interests lie? The situation was fraught with peril and conflict. *"Quis custodiet ipsos custodes?"* wrote the Roman satirist Juvenal. Who will guard the guardians?

Some would argue that the market eventually took care of the problem. Enron and its auditor are out of business. But at what cost? Thousands of Enron employees lost their jobs and millions of investors lost their savings. Should they have known better than to trust Enron's board, rated one of the best in the world? Yes, the "bad guys" got taken down, but the collateral damage was horrific. Enron failed because its senior leaders did not understand the Integrity-Performance Paradox. They traded the truth for quarterly numbers.

Taking Action

How do we take responsibility for our actions and ensure that we honestly represent the performance and risks of our enterprises?

Though we oath takers do not claim to be experts possessed of years of wisdom or experience, a few things appear quite obvious to us. We need to be aware of the line dividing bluff from bald-faced lies. We need to at least ask the question "Is this a permissible negotiation bluff, or is this a fraudulent representation of the quality of the goods or services we offer?" We should also be attuned to our instinct to avoid failure at all costs. We should find a way to face our fear of failure and deal with it realistically and honestly—both with ourselves and others. We need to create transparency, and simultaneously learn to live and work within an inevitable tension.

Michael Beer, in his book on business ethics, *High Commitment, High Performance,* speaks to the importance of transparency within a company. Beer posited three core reasons why Wall Street failed so badly in the fall of 2008. One of the key failings was the inability of actors inside large banks to speak truth to power. Key players felt intimidated by superiors. The internal voice of conscience was silenced by a maniacal focus on short-term profits and uncritical acceptance of whatever scheme might bring them in. The silencing of employees who sought to challenge strategy and risk-management practices likely undermined whatever moral authority might have existed. It emboldened those who already felt inclined to do the wrong thing. If you cannot speak hard truth to those with whom you work, even those who supervise you, then you operate in a haze of "yes-ism." You collaborate with silent deceit in the way that an enabler silently collaborates with an alcoholic. An alcoholic-like haze of denial permeates the atmosphere of the office.

To create an honest external reporting culture in your firm, you need to have honesty within the firm. Warren Bennis and James O'Toole have written extensively on the topic of transparency.

Their advice to businesses is to push for as much transparency within their firms as possible. "Because no organization can be honest with the public if it is not honest with itself," they write, "we define transparency broadly, as the degree to which information flows freely within an organization, among managers and employees, and outward to stakeholders."[10] Bennis and O'Toole describe real-world company-wide transparency in the example of SRC Holdings, a remanufacturing company in Springfield, Missouri. "For the past twenty years," Bennis observed, "every employee at SRC . . . has had access to all financial and managerial information, and each is taught how to interpret and apply it. The net effect, in the words of the company's CFO, 'is like having seven hundred internal auditors out there in every function of the company.'"[11]

Another way to boost transparency is to reward dissension. Several business leaders have already taken creative approaches. At Motorola, for example, Robert Galvin financially rewarded contrarians and made it part of the review process; at Northrop Grumman, Frank Daly taught employees to practice difficult conversations, so that when the time came to have a real one, they could be ready. Bennis stresses the importance of diversifying your sources of information—in essence, actively seek out people who may dissent with you. "When you're setting out to understand a culture, it's best to seek diverse sources of information that demonstrate a variety of biases. This is a simple and obvious point, but rare is the leader who regularly meets with—and listens to—employees, reporters, shareholders, regulators, and even annoying critics."[12]

Regardless of whether you work for an energy company or an apple juice manufacturer, you will face the temptation to fudge the truth or go along with the flow of dangerous practices. One of the reasons, we have seen, is an unwillingness to accept the tension that is a natural part of dissent and dealing with the truth head-on. We must be willing to endure the tension, despite the discomfort it gives. During the civil rights era of the 1960s, Martin Luther King Jr. was accused of creating tension and discord. His response is notable for its directness and common sense:

> . . . We who engage in nonviolent direct action are not the creators of tension. We merely bring to the surface the hidden tension that is already alive. We bring it out in the open, where it can be seen and dealt with. Like a boil that can never be cured so long as it is covered up but must be opened with . . . its ugliness to the natural medicines of air and light, injustice must be exposed, with all the tension its exposure creates, to the light of human conscience and the air of national opinion before it can be cured.[13]

King understood that problems would not go away by ignoring them. The same is true in business—problems do not just go away quietly. They become subtle fault lines that will erupt in dangerous collisions of moving forces in due time. Adulterated apple juice will eventually be discovered. Deceitful accounting practices will be revealed in public and in courts of law.

A manager leads by example. What is true for leading an organization is also true for leading oneself. Restructuring a corporation may require restructuring our own lives first. This is what the oath is all about. It's an act of commitment and willingness to examine and change fault-line behaviors. Peter Andersen operated in isolation. When trouble came, like a spooked horse, he took off running. When we are tempted to do that, we need to make sure that we are not running away from our problems but are instead running toward the truth.

David Hobbet, a signer of the MBA Oath from Kellogg School of Management at Northwestern University, offers,

> For me, my pledge to "take responsibility for my actions, and represent the performance and risks of my enterprise accurately and honestly" is most relevant in the day-to-day minutiae of business. When my boss asks about a product launch date that I know is at risk, will I reply, "We're on track"? When asked if a new project "has everyone's buy-in," will I gloss over a recent debate or accurately represent the ongoing disagreement? Even more so, what if the honest answer paints my performance in a negative light? After all, the main reason this tenet is needed is that sometimes the honest answer *does* paint our performance or the performance of our enterprise in a negative light.
>
> The only way is to get very comfortable being honest in the day-to-day, even if it means hindering my own career. It means continually being forthright, even when a half-truth would be more convenient, and asking my peers to hold me accountable to doing just that. This is not always easy.

Indeed, when you take responsibility for your actions, it is not always easy. And yet, if you are honest about the risks and actual performance, you achieve a certain peace, one that allows you to sleep well at night and not awake in fear in the morning. You do not fear being found out. You live without being afraid of losing the admiration of others. You act with humility and a deep sense of integrity. You are finally on the path to becoming a true leader.

11

PERSONAL AND PROFESSIONAL
GROWTH

I will develop both myself and other managers under my
supervision so that the profession continues to grow and
contribute to the well-being of society.

MBA Oath, Sixth Promise

The oath is a formal statement of what we believe in. With
knowledge and learning comes responsibility. After going
through rigorous training in Business, Management, and
Leadership, we have no excuse to be complacent.

—Shamshad Khan, Thunderbird School of Global Management,
Class of 2009, signer #1363

I t feels like life temporarily just turned into a sitcom. We've
been working at Max's apartment building, which has a public
solarium on the top floor with a great view of New York City. It
is a great place to write. There is something calming about looking at the madness of Manhattan from above. Tonight we had our
laptops open and notes spread on a table when two middle-aged
couples walked in to admire the view. One couple had just moved
into the building, and they were showing their friends around.
One of the men waved at us to get our attention.

"Hey there, what are you up to?" He was wearing a black leather jacket with an elastic waist and was chewing gum.

"We're just doing some writing," Max answered, hoping brevity would somehow portray the idea that we were men who were in deep thought and should not be disturbed. It did not work.

"Oh yeah?" the man's wife said. "What is it, a book? I'm a writer."

"Really?" Peter smiled. Might as well be polite. "Yeah, it's a book."

"What's it about?" the man asked.

"It's about business ethics," Max replied. Both couples spontaneously broke into laughter.

"That's rich," the second man said. "What is it, a work of fiction?" The couples guffawed again. It felt like we were being taped before a live studio audience.

The first man replied, "No, it's a book about the concept of oxymorons." Again, laughter. The first man then grabbed some more gum, passed it around, and the couples exited stage right.

Further evidence on a Thursday evening that things need to change.

———

When prospective students apply to business school they often mention the motivation to utilize their MBA schooling as a period of contemplation; to assume a different vantage point and reflect on where they want their careers to go. We both, thousands of miles apart and writing separately before we had ever met, wrote about it in our applications. Peter called it the "mountaintop experience to gain perspective." And yes, it does sound cheesy to us in hindsight.

In many ways, the MBA experience is about ushering in a deeper period of thoughtfulness about life. For bankers and consultants, business school is an opportunity to consider more specific, operationally focused career destinations. For a student coming from the military, it is an opportunity to consider the numerous options in the private sector. From the moment you begin to write your first application essay, to your first steps on campus, to the day you graduate, business school is an opportunity to reflect. To breathe different air. And yet, why does this thoughtfulness, this investment in renewal, have to be confined to two years on campus?

The sixth promise of the MBA Oath is a pledge that, as managers, we will continually develop in order to bring our most informed judgment to bear in making decisions for our organizations and the societies in which we operate. How will we be informed if we are not constantly learning? How will we grow if we do not develop the disciplined habit of listening to and learning from others? Management, as a practice, does not easily adhere to laboratory tests and written examinations. You cannot learn it like surgery or engineering. It is a practice and you learn by experience. Some leadership development experts say that 70 percent of a person's leadership development occurs on the job, 20 percent as a result of coach-led facilitating experiences, and only 10 percent in the classroom. This suggests there is a lot to learn after you take your last standardized exam and receive your diploma. As professionals, we MBAs should strive to make our judgments informed by never ceasing to educate ourselves. Furthermore, we ought to follow a principle of renewal personally, corporately, and as a profession.

Personal Development and Renewal

When he was well into his nineties, John Gardner once gave a speech on the subject of personal renewal to his old colleagues at McKinsey & Company. Gardner had been a senior director at the firm and had served in the State Department. We read his speech in preparation for the last class we ever had at business school. After more than four hundred cases, our professors handed us Gardner's speech as a capstone case study. Looking back on his years in business, Gardner reflected on the importance of renewing oneself. He began his talk by referencing an article he read on barnacles. It was a peculiar start to a speech and we admit it is a peculiar portion of a speech to quote, but we think it has great meaning.

> "The barnacle" the author explained, "is confronted with an existential decision about where it's going to live. Once it decides . . . it spends the rest of its life with its head cemented to a rock." End of quote. For a good many of us, it comes to that . . . I'm not talking about people who fail to get to the top in achievement. We can't all get to the top, and that isn't the point of life anyway. I'm talking about people who—no matter how busy they seem to be—have stopped learning or growing . . . We can't write off the danger of complacency, growing rigidity, imprisonment by our own comfortable habits and opinions.[1]

Bored, complacent, going through the motions: Gardner's description of the danger of becoming a barnacle sounds familiar. We all have probably seen it firsthand in bosses, colleagues, or family members who seem dulled by the drudgery of their work. We can already imagine it in the lives of classmates who take jobs because of security rather than personal interest. There is nothing wrong with taking a job that is a stepping-stone to another, or a job that provides stability, but we should keep in mind that we are making existential decisions similar to that of the barnacle.

How do we avoid spending the rest of our life with our head cemented to a rock? Probably few of us anticipate ever reaching that point of complacency in our lives. That is why we were surprised to read Gardner's diagnosis of what causes the barnacle syndrome. For many people, it occurs not just because we get sedentary but also because we move too fast.

> One of the enemies of sound, lifelong motivation is a rather childish conception we have of the kind of concrete, describable goal toward which all of our efforts drive us. We want to believe that there is a point at which we can feel that we have arrived. We want a scoring system that tells us when we've piled up enough points to count ourselves successful . . . So you scramble and sweat and climb to reach what you thought was the goal. When you get to the top you stand up and look around and chances are you feel a little empty. Maybe more than a little empty . . . You wonder whether you climbed the wrong mountain . . . But life isn't a mountain that has a summit. Nor is it—as some suppose—a riddle that has an answer. Nor a game that has a final score.[2]

Gardner's words add another element to our reflection on ambition from a previous chapter. Not only can trying to reach the summit blind you to your duties to other climbers on the mountain, it can prevent you from developing yourself. The mountaintop experience you are seeking might not be as fulfilling as you had hoped. *Have I climbed the wrong mountain?* What a horrible thought, made the worse if there was no joy in the climb itself. Yet it does not have to be so. As any mountaineer knows, the summit is exhilarating, but the journey should be enjoyed. There are places along the climb that can be just as beautiful as the peak. The climb itself ought to be renewing.

Stephen R. Covey begins the final chapter in his book on the habits of successful people with a brief story:

> Suppose you were to come upon someone in the woods working feverishly to saw down a tree.
>
> "What are you doing?" you ask.
>
> "Can't you see?" comes the impatient reply. "I'm sawing down this tree."
>
> "You look exhausted!" you exclaim. "How long have you been at it?"
>
> "Over five hours," he returns, "and I'm beat! This is hard work."
>
> "Well, why don't you take a break for a few minutes and sharpen that saw?" you inquire. "I'm sure it would go a lot faster."
>
> "I don't have time to sharpen the saw," the man says emphatically. "I'm too busy sawing!"[3]

The lesson is clear: in order to be effective at what you do, you need time away from what you do for renewal. Renewal can mean a time of rest to regain perspective; it can also mean purposeful time to pursue new knowledge. To borrow from Covey, it means to "sharpen the saw" so that we are getting the most out of the most effective tool we have—ourselves. It is a principle that runs throughout life. Race cars need pit stops, weight lifters need breaks between sets, and soil needs time between plantings to yield a healthy crop.

A key to personal career growth then is to enjoy the journey but avoid the false belief in a final destination. In the fall of our second year at business school, Michael Dell came to campus. A student in the audience asked about his legacy: How did he want to be remembered? Without skipping a beat, Dell said, "Sam Walton opened his first Walmart when he was forty-three. I am forty-two. So, it's still early days." Admire Dell or not, this was from a man who had started a company at nineteen, ran it for twenty-odd years, became a billionaire, left his company to "retire," and was now back as CEO running daily activities. You could sense his resolve in helping steer Dell Computer toward its next destination. For Dell, becoming a billionaire was no summit. It was another stop on his personal journey.

The important lesson is that we should not be climbing just to reach the top of the corporate ladder. We should climb because *the climb itself engages us.* Why should a second-year associate at a consulting firm work hard and do a good job? Because she wants to make partner? Or because the work is worth doing well in its own right? These two reasons are not mutually exclusive, but from what we hear from MBA friends, the emphasis is often heavily on the former reason. Yet we should be motivated by the opportunities for personal growth—whether we are in fledgling post-MBA jobs or are decades into our careers.

The poet David Whyte explores these themes in seminars he conducts for corporate leaders on business and poetry. He emphasizes what we feel to be true—that as professionals looking to make a real impact, we need to deeply believe that what we are doing is of true worth. "To feel that what we do is right for ourselves and good for the world at the exact same time—is one of the great triumphs of human existence. We do feel, when we have work that is challenging and enlarging and that seems to be doing something for others, as if . . . we could move mountains, as if we could call the world *home*; and for a while, in our imaginations, no matter the small size of our apartment, we dwell in a spacious house with endless horizons."[4]

You can either climb mountains or you can move mountains. The key is to work for the sake of the work itself, not just for the sake of future reward. Whyte's idea is really an Aristotelian notion that good work and the good life is like an archer hitting the mark. In Aristotle's opinion, we ought to think about the kind of person we really want to be and work toward becoming that ideal, as well as we can. We ought to take our experiences and reflect on them as lessons to teach us about ourselves. That is the requirement for renewal and growth.

Scott Snook makes the analogy to watching a film. Your experience of a movie differs depending on whether you read reviews of the film beforehand or not, or whether you go out for coffee afterward and discuss it with friends. "While the movie itself was objectively the same stimulus for everyone in that theater, what dozens of moviegoers did with that experience after leaving no doubt influenced their overall experience. In one sense, the movie didn't end with the credits."[5] Snook argues that professionally, most people tend to focus on what "movies" they select to watch (where will they work, in what role, etc.) and largely ignore the significance of preparation and reflection in determining their experience of work. Just as a movie has less meaning if we reflect on it less, work has less meaning if we just experience it as a way to fill our calendars and do not reflect on what it has to teach us about ourselves and the world.

Research done by the Center for Creative Leadership suggests that personal growth requires reflection, but reflection is precisely what time-crunched leaders lack most. One of the best questions we heard at business school was directed at the CEO of Danaher Corporation, Lawrence Culp. A student asked, "If you had an extra hour in the day, where would you spend it?" No matter the answer, it's a worthwhile question to ask. Leadership researcher Morgan McCall writes, "The best executives aren't necessarily managers who possess a previously identified, generic list of traits or who have risen to the top through survival of the fittest. Rather, the real leaders of the future are those who have the ability to learn from their experiences and remain open to continuous learning."[6] Based on a study of some of the most successful managers in the United States. McCall and colleagues determined that the single most useful predictor of an executive's success is the executive's tenacity in extracting something worthwhile from their experience, whatever the experience is. Reflection is renewing because it gives you perspective on your experiences. It allows you to digest them so they become the food for your growth.

Personal renewal through reflection is key to avoiding the life of a barnacle, to working for the joy of the work itself, not just for future reward. One creative way of helping yourself with this is to consciously develop a group of close friends to help you. Just as companies have boards of directors who oversee the performance and management of the company, you can have a personal board of directors who accept a duty to advise you on the performance and management of your life. Kennedy had his kitchen cabinet. Arthur had his round table. What would it look like if we had personal boards of directors who gave support and advice on tough questions? We hope that the MBA Oath community, as it grows, can help foster accountability toward continuous learning and personal renewal.

Ultimately, the responsibility for personal renewal and development is yours. Bill George conducted first-person interviews with 125 of today's top leaders. His research led him to conclude that "to be an effective leader, *you must take responsibility for your own development.*" Only you will ensure that your saw is sharp. Kroger CEO David Dillon told him that most people he has seen develop as good leaders were self-taught. "The advice I give to individuals in our company is not to expect the company to hand you a development plan that will take care of everything. You need to take responsibility for developing yourself."[7] Dillon's advice for his employees is to look out for themselves. However, even in giving them that advice, Dillon is looking out for them, which brings us to the second part of this pledge—*organizational* development and renewal.

Organizational Development and Renewal

As we put together the MBA Oath in the spring of 2009 and discussed this tenet on development, we decided that in addition to developing ourselves, we ought to go a step further and work to help other managers develop as well. In fact, the more we think about it, pushing our organizations to learn seems less like a good idea and more like a strategic imperative. The importance is well summarized by Ray Stata, former CEO of Analog Devices: "The rate at which individuals and organizations learn may well become the only sustainable competitive advantage." One of our professors, David Garvin, reminds us that products and services can be copied. Even processes can be copied—six sigma is available on the open market. But if you're learning more rapidly than the competition, you can get and stay ahead. More than that, the world is changing rapidly. We have a more global environment, deregulation, and new business models. If your rate of learning is not greater than that rate of change, you are going to fall behind.[8]

Garvin has coined the term "learning oganization" to describe enterprises that learn effectively. He says there are three building blocks of any learning organization. First, learning organizations have a *supportive learning environment.* Employees feel safe disagreeing with others, asking naive questions, and owning up to mistakes. They recognize the value of opposing ideas and take risks to explore the unknown. One example is Children's Hospital and Clinics in Minnesota, which instituted a policy of "blameless reporting." Employees began identifying and reporting risks without fear of blame. And the number of preventable deaths and illnesses decreased.[9]

Second, learning organizations have a *concrete learning process* for generating, collecting, interpreting, and disseminating information. They gather intelligence on competitors, customers, and technological trends; identify and solve problems; and develop employees' skills. The U.S. Army has an After Action Review process that exemplifies this. After every mission or project, they hold a systematic debriefing process in which participants ask (1) What did we set out to do? (2) What actually happened? (3) Why? (4) What should we do next time? The results are shared widely and quickly.[10]

Finally, learning organizations have *leaders that reinforce learning.* Their leaders are willing to entertain alternative viewpoints, engage in active questioning and listening, and signal the importance of spending time on reflection. Harvey Golub, the former CEO of American Express, challenged managers to think creatively by asking them such questions as "What alternatives have you considered?" and "What are your premises?"[11] This is not rocket science, but it does require managers to go a step beyond command and control leadership to get their people to think more deeply about why they are doing what they are doing.

Just as important as getting their people to reflect, leaders should aspire to coach and teach their people to *act* in courageous and ethical ways. General Electric has rising leaders go through simulations where they are forced to choose between doing a big profitable deal and doing the right thing. The company's commitment to scenario-based ethics training helps employees articulate their perspectives prior to the challenge. Former GE CEO Jack Welch was hyper-competitive about winning, but he was just as adamant that his leaders did things the right way. At GE's training center in Crotonville, New York, he would bark, "If you really win by cheating—by gaming the system, or fudging the numbers, or skirting some standard or ordinance—you didn't win, and you will not be successful in GE."[12] Messages like that, made by one of the most successful CEOs of the century, make an impression. It is important for us to hear those messages, not just from our professors or from our fellow students but from top leaders. When we hear the message from Jack Welch, we have to pay attention.

American Express, the U.S. Army, and GE are huge organizations that have created learning environments, but a learning organization could just as well be a small company or even a group within a larger organization. As managers we can, and should, start with our own groups. Start with your own behavior and lead by example. Show curiosity. Ask questions. Admit when you are confused. Look for opportunities to mentor and coach.

If you have made it to business school, we guarantee that you had the help of a few good mentors along the way. You may have also picked up new mentors while you were at school. What makes them special? Why have they been influential in your life? The two of us have mentors from school who tell us they will always pick up the phone when we call, despite how busy they are. And they are as good as their word. What if every MBA became a mentor like that? How many millions of people would flourish as a result? This is the kind of leadership that creates the environment in which learning organizations can thrive and where individuals themselves can develop and grow.

Professional Development and Renewal

We have discussed personal renewal and corporate renewal. Expanding our circle further, we turn now to professional renewal. This pledge is as much about contributing to the strength of the profession as it is about developing oneself and one's organization. The commitment by managers to grow their profession and to contribute to the well-being of society implicitly means looking beyond oneself to the actions of others, especially those with whom one works.

Where do we start? We have a simple and straightforward recommendation. We MBAs ought to consider making continuing education a requirement of holding the degree. Both lawyers and doctors are required to complete a certain number of continuing education credits each year in order to maintain their licenses. Why not make a similar requirement for MBAs? There would be benefits for shareholders, for schools, and for ourselves. First, shareholders would benefit because it would mean their managers are more educated on the issues of the day. What if every director of a corporate board were required to know something about derivatives? Might they have been better equipped to deal with the recent financial crisis as it unfolded? Our innovations got ahead of our understanding of them. Alan Greenspan wrote in the *Wall Street Journal*, "It is now very clear that the levels of complexity to which market practitioners at the height of their euphoria tried to push risk-management techniques and products were too much for even the most sophisticated market players to handle properly and prudently."[13] They ignored the risk, until they could not ignore it any more. Like law or medicine, the field of knowledge in business changes quickly, perhaps more quickly because of the breadth of the field. Shareholders should demand that the leaders and directors of their firms are educated and competent to deal with the risks of the corporation.

Business schools would also benefit from making continuing education a mandatory part of joining a society of MBAs for a very different and very simple reason: more income. Continuing education requirements increase lifetime customer value. "Customers" whom they currently only have for one or two years could bring repeat business every eighteen to twenty-four months. Already, some business schools make more money from their executive education program than they do from the MBA program. Continuing education credits might be even more profitable because they could come in the form of one-to-many videos or Web conferences.

Finally, MBAs would benefit too. Like the MBA itself, continuing education classes would provide opportunities to meet peers and learn from each other. More important, it would help restore respect to the degree. By engaging in continuing education, MBAs would make a statement that says, "We care so much about leading responsibly that we are willing to take on these extra education obligations." Such a commitment would show real leadership.

The MBA Oath's commitment to professional development is a commitment to inform your judgment and stay abreast of the evolving knowledge in your field. It is not enough to blindly trust in the latest fads of investing. You need to know enough to evaluate with a critical eye. We need to hone the clarity of our sight by investing in ourselves, our organizations, and our community of managerial colleagues. If we do, then we have the potential to make a real difference in the world. And in the future, when we mention the phrase "business ethics" to a stranger there is less of a chance we will feel like we are in a sitcom.

12

SUSTAINING PROSPERITY
AND LIVING WELL

I will strive to create sustainable economic, social, and environmental prosperity worldwide. Sustainable prosperity is created when the enterprise produces an output in the long run that is greater than the opportunity cost of all the inputs it consumes.

MBA Oath, Seventh Promise

Some of the most important increases in the living standards around the world have been as a result of the capitalistic pursuit of profit, and the oath seeks to maximize the good that can be created through sustainable business enterprises, and minimize unsustainable exploitation of our planet, its resources, or its people.

Kevin Meyers, Harvard, Class of 2009,
signer #51

Manville Corporation was a Denver-based company that had a tragic knack for making extremely popular industrial products that later turned out to be extraordinarily dangerous for public health. In the midseventies, asbestos accounted for half of the firm's profits. However, the product, as Manville's medical director later described it, was "the worst occupational health disaster ever known to any company in the free world." By inhaling asbestos fibers used in home insulation (among other applications), thousands of people contracted fatal cancer. The company itself did not escape the health damage from its product. Entire departments full of people at Manville's asbestos plant in Waukegan, Illinois, died from asbestos-related cancer. In the 1980s, asbestos lawsuits mounted against the company. Eventually, Manville's predicted asbestos liability grew to $2 billion, a crushing figure. Thus in 1982, the Manville Corporation became the largest U.S. industrial company ever to file for Chapter 11 bankruptcy.[1]

The company reorganized and chose Tom Stephens to be the new CEO. On his shoulders rested the burden of leading the company out of bankruptcy. As part of the reorganization, the court prevented future lawsuits against Manville by making all asbestos claimants part of two trusts that would own four-fifths of Manville stock and have representatives sit on Manville's board. Therefore, Stephens's responsibility to create returns for shareholders had special significance—he was helping the families of victims who had their lives taken by the company's product.

Manville's reemergence came largely on the back of one product: fiberglass. Like asbestos, it was initially hailed as a miracle product. In 1986, Manville sold $807 million worth of it. Representing 75 percent of the company's profits, fiberglass was used as insulation in 99 percent of new housing starts that year.

Because of Manville's past, members of the company were more committed to safety than were most firms. Bill Sells, head of the fiberglass division, had been a manager in the Waukegan asbestos plant and seen many of his own people die of cancer. "No one, till the day I die," Sells said, "can take out of me the belief I have in industry's need for product stewardship."[2] As a result, Manville subjected its new material to rigorous testing. As of 1986, fiberglass was the most widely studied industrial material in the world. More than forty thousand fiberglass workers had been studied, and no carcinogenic link had been discovered under normal levels of exposure. However, none of these studies could be conclusive about the long-term effects. As with asbestos, the challenge with fiberglass contamination was that it could take up to twenty years to witness the effects in the human body.

Then in 1986, almost out of nowhere, Sir Richard Doll, an academic researcher studying asbestos, triggered a trying period of decision making for Manville's executive team. Doll concluded a World Health Organization symposium on man-made mineral fibers by speculating, based on incomplete scientific data, that fiberglass could be as dangerous as asbestos. This new study was incomplete and used only the "crudest tools and measurements," but because of Manville's history, no one in the company could ignore it. It was like déjà vu all over again.

If you were Tom Stephens, what would you do? Pull the product from the market? Fund further research on fiberglass? Relabel it with a cancer-hazard warning? You have five thousand employees working at the company's fifteen fiberglass manufacturing plants to think about. You are responsible for them. You also have ten thousand asbestos victims who own your company through the bankruptcy trusts to think about. If you pull the product, what happens to them? You will not have conclusive evidence for years, but you have to make a decision in the interim. On one hand, if you go public with the information, you could face a PR disaster despite uncertainty around health risk. On the other hand, if you do nothing and wait twenty years to obtain conclusive evidence, thousands of people could die, just like what happened with asbestos. How do you create any prosperity in a situation like that?

=====

In his book *If Aristotle Ran General Motors,* philosopher Tom Morris applies Aristotle's thinking about politics to business. In *The Politics,* Aristotle explores basic questions about why cities exist. Why, he asked, do people live together and work together instead of going through life alone? It is an interesting question. Aristotle concluded that the city is "a partnership for living well."[3] That is the ultimate purpose of cities. People come together so they can *prosper,* so they can *flourish.* Likewise, Morris explains, a business is more than a building, or equipment, or organizational charts. It is a partnership of people creating a better life for themselves and for others. "If Aristotle ran General Motors, everyone employed there would think of it as one huge partnership, encompassing myriads of smaller partnerships, for the purpose of living well." Morris continues, "We should always be asking ourselves whether what we contemplate doing will enhance or diminish this crucial function of the business within our own domain of influence. Are we building partnerships for living well?"[4]

We signed the MBA Oath because at the end of the day, we believe whether we are in business or not, whether we sign the oath or not, we all ought to strive to create sustainable economic, social, and environmental prosperity. We think of the seventh promise of the MBA Oath the way Aristotle might; we think of it as a commitment to engage in a partnership for living well. We seek to make profits because we think it builds to the goal of living well. We seek to protect the vulnerable around us because that is part of living well. We seek to preserve our environment because seeing it flourish is also part of what it means to live well.

Prosperity can be defined as a state of flourishing, thriving, success, or good fortune. Our contemporary notion of prosperity has shrunken to the size of our own pocketbooks; we think of it mostly in terms of wealth, but we could enlarge our vision of prosperity to mean flourishing in every sense. We could think of it more broadly as the state of living well. Living well economically. Living well socially. Living well environmentally. Ultimately, that is the greatest justification for business—to enter into a partnership for living well.

A lot of social debate revolves around pitting one of these three elements of prosperity—economic, social, and environmental—in a zero-sum struggle against the other two. We remember growing up and hearing about the controversy over the northern spotted owl. The owl was on the endangered species list and was supposed to be protected, so the government proposed a moratorium on logging in the owl's habitat. As a result, the logging industry was infuriated, claiming tens of thousands of jobs would be lost. Pro-logging protesters created bumper stickers like "Kill a spotted owl—Save a Logger" and "I like spotted owls—fried."[5] On the other hand, environmentalists claimed that the owl was symbolic of a greater ecosystem at risk. Saving the owl would save countless other environmental treasures. It was a battle between economic prosperity and environmental prosperity.

These battles carry on. China is the most notable case today. Over the last thirty years, China has achieved an annual growth rate of 9 percent as its economy has doubled in size every eight years. Today, China exports more in a single day than it did in all of 1978. And the human story has been breathtaking. The average income for the Chinese has increased sevenfold. In thirty years, four hundred million people have moved out of abject poverty.[6] The growth in China's economic prosperity is phenomenal and has occurred at a pace never before seen. However, China's rapid industrialization has come at the cost of severe environmental degradation. China is home to eighteen of the twenty most polluted cities in the world. The country's environmental protection agency estimates that 45 percent of the rivers and waterways it monitors are unsuitable for human contact. Now the country faces an estimated more than *fifty thousand* environment-related protests per year, and some of them have grown violent.[7]

We accept that some of these conflicts between social, economic, and environmental prosperity are inevitable. Although it would be nice if we could always pursue strategies that lead to prosperity in all three dimensions at the same time, leaders of firms and of nations cannot always have it all. Sometimes leaders will have to prioritize one over the other. Chris Palo, an MBA and oath signer from Drexel University, writes, "As a single manager, how can I influence sustainable prosperity worldwide? The world's a mighty large place and not every MBA graduate will be the CEO of a transnational corporation. But every manager does affect their circle of cohorts, employees, and society. So as a signer of the MBA Oath, it is my responsibility not only to take sustainability seriously, but also help *create* sustainability to the best of my power." Everyone should do what they can.

By arguing for social and environmental prosperity, we are not saying that companies should give away their profits or that we should transfer wealth from shareholders to third parties. Four hundred million Chinese did not move out of poverty due to simple charity. They did it by building an economy, one that is increasingly capitalistic. The hopes of the global poor depend on economic growth and upon business leaders creating value and growth responsibly. When an economy is in a recession, few people will rise from poverty. It is only through growth and the creation of new opportunity that their fortunes will change. Similarly, the hope for a sustainably healthy environment depends first on people being able to meet their basic economic needs.

The seventh promise of the MBA Oath challenges us to pursue prosperity in the threefold sense. We ought to be capitalists, but capitalists with a conscience. We ought to see in our work the opportunity to play a part in addressing the great problems facing the world. The world is constantly falling apart. It is broken like a piece of pottery. Working for prosperity is more than picking up the pieces and gluing them together again. It is spinning new clay and reworking it to make it stronger. We ought not only work for our own prosperity, but also see in our success the opportunity to create prosperity for others.

Going deeper, what does sustainable prosperity look like economically, socially, and environmentally? We will here offer a few thoughts on each.

Economic Prosperity

Of the three types of sustainability we mention, economic prosperity is the least controversial. We imagine economic prosperity as a state of growth with rising profits and full employment. Who does not want *that*? And who does not want to sustain it? Economic prosperity is sustainable when enterprises produce an economic output in the long run that is greater than the opportunity cost of all the inputs it consumes. It is sustainable when the boom and busts of overleverage and investment are moderated and mellowed. As the years of 2008 and 2009 depicted, we have a long way to go. We think two orienting concepts are useful for building toward a more sustainable economic prosperity: good-enough returns and long-term value.

When you bet it all, you do not always win. In the past two decades, too many people got too comfortable with the idea that "the more you bet, the more you win when you win." Too few learned until 2008 that trying to get excessive wins exposes you to excessive losses. Maybe prosperity looks different from this. Maybe it looks like "good-enough" returns. This is the first orienting concept we propose for sustainable economic prosperity. Investor Howard Marks has commented that "there should be a point at which investors decline to take more risk in the pursuit of more return, because they are satisfied with the return they expect and would rather achieve that with high confidence than try for more at the risk of falling short (or losing money) . . . Less gain, perhaps, but also less pain."[8] Maybe we are better off when we balance risk and return rather than trying to maximize. Maybe our companies would be more stable, jobs more predictable, our economies more steady. We should consider this approach.

The second orienting concept for building sustainable economic prosperity is creating long-term value. Why? Every discounted cash flow analysis we modeled in business school assumed an ongoing terminal value. Sometimes an outsized majority of a company's value was baked in to the terminal value assumptions. Companies are valued as going concerns. We need to manage them as such. Recently, business luminaries, including Warren Buffett and Bill George, signed a document compiled by the Aspen Institute entitled "Overcoming Short-termism," advocating for a wiser, more patient approach to creating value. Creating

long-term value means overcoming the perverse incentives created by short-termism. A middle manager in a corporation may
make decisions that will affect the health of the company for
years even though she may move on and never experience the
consequences. When Manville faced its second major crisis, Tom
Stephens had to consider the long-term consequences of whatever decision he made. Economic prosperity in firms and economies will only be sustainable when we keep the long-term at the
forefront of our decisions.

Social Prosperity

What is social prosperity? It is when society is left better off
because of the existence of a company. In other words, society
will benefit in the form of meaningful employment for people
and products that increase quality of life. It is when the output
of a company is worth more than the social inputs it consumes.
It is when a firm at worst does no harm and at best enhances
the human dignity of the people and communities it affects. The
question is how to determine the boundaries of responsibility.
Are you responsible just for your customers? What about the
people in the town where your factory is? What about the people
affected by the employment conditions in your supply chain at
companies you do not own? Where do you draw the line?

Jacques Zwahlen found himself asking this question over
breakfast one morning in 2004. Zwahlen was CEO of Charles
Veillon, a large Swiss mail-order catalog company. He was listening to the radio when he heard a story about an international
children's rights group accusing Swedish retailer IKEA of selling handwoven carpets made in South Asia by children working

under horrible conditions. Zwahlen shuddered. Just in the last quarter, his firm too had added a line of handwoven carpets from South Asia to his catalog. Zwahlen called his carpet buyer to inquire into whether child workers were producing the carpets. Three of the four suppliers refused to give information about their labor sources.

Zwahlen immediately made the decision to end his company's relationship with the three suppliers and look for alternatives. Maybe this is what anyone would do in the same position. After hearing the report about IKEA, he recognized the public relations business risk of having the same practices in his own company, and he trembled on a human level as he thought about the children. But Zwahlen intuited that the children were working under these conditions for a reason—they needed money and this was the best alternative. If his firm boycotted the carpets, and those factories shut down as a result, the child workers might be driven to other, possibly more damaging, occupations. Simply pulling out could decimate their prospects without providing alternatives. Zwahlen consulted a child welfare organization to learn about other ways his business could improve the conditions of child laborers. Over time, Zwahlen's company engaged in a new program of monitoring supplier working conditions and launched an experimental program that combined education with work benefits for children in the South Asian carpet industry.[9]

Zwahlen's actions became widely reported and he was soon asked for an interview on a well-known French television program. At the end of a lengthy discussion of the child labor issue, the host asked Zwahlen, "What motivates you? Is it, so to speak, a feeling of world citizenship, a humanitarian instinct, or is it also a necessary business precaution to work like this because if anyone ever found out, you would be ruined?" Zwahlen refused to choose between one or the other. He replied, "It's both, I think." The host then suggested "that we take the cynical position for a moment." Zwahlen again refused. "No. First, it's intolerable from a humanist point of view to imagine participating in a destructive economic practice, leading nowhere, which does nothing for the communities which practice it, nor for their countries, nor for the consumer country. So the humanitarian aspect is there, but behind it, one must realize that . . . a company caught participating in this type of commerce risks losing its reputation."[10]

Zwahlen refused to be cast in the role of an angel. He made his decision both for humanitarian reasons *and* because it was the best thing for his company. It was not either-or, it was both-and. We agree. We are moral beings and we have fundamental duties to each other that supersede even our vocational responsibilities, but it is not enough to simply pursue our values: we need to recognize the real business consequences of our action and inaction. We should seek to create social prosperity, but we must necessarily pursue economic prosperity as well. This both-and approach is the standard to which we aspire.

Environmental Prosperity

The third lens of our focus on prosperity is the environment. Growing up in Colorado and Hawaii, we understood the outdoors as our respective states' greatest resources. It attracts tourism and provides a wonderful quality of life for those of us fortunate to live in areas rich with expansive forests, mountains, and rivers. We grew up thinking we should treat our natural resources with the utmost care and that there are more opportunities than costs for business when it comes to protecting our environment. The trouble with a phrase like "environmental prosperity" is that people can interpret it in many different ways. Some have questioned whether we are trying to smuggle in some extremist idea that big business is bad and that we should never harm a blade of grass. We are simply arguing that we ought to try to protect the right of future generations to enjoy a planet that is clean and resource rich.

So what do we think environmental prosperity means? A friend, Timothy J. Keller, makes the analogy to gardening. When you are a gardener, you are neither a park ranger nor a steam-roller. The park ranger runs around telling people not to touch anything. The steamroller touches everything and paves over it. The gardener is different. He takes the raw material of the world and rearranges it to grow food and provide for human flourish-ing. The goal of the gardener is to make things flourish. The vegetation in his garden flourishes. The people he feeds flourish. He alters the landscape in some ways, but he does so respectfully and with great care. That is environmental prosperity.

The truth is we think this is an opportunity like never before since the creation of capitalism to unite sustainably profitable businesses with sustainable environmental initiatives. Many busi-nesses today are combining their concern for environmental and economic prosperity into amazingly creative, sustainable, and profitable business models. One such company is RecycleBank, which creates marketing partnerships with such retailers as Rite-Aid, Whole Foods, and Chik-fil-A to offer rewards points to households for recycling more. RecycleBank measures how much you recycle with RFID tags attached to your recycling containers. You earn points for your efforts and redeem them at over two thousand retailers. Not every business will be so environment-centric, but every business should be environmentally friendly. We mean *every* business. If the world's largest retailer can be, then any business can.

Walmart shoppers expect to see everyday low prices when they look at items on the shelves. Soon they will also see the environmental impact of every one of those items as well. The $400 billion retail giant is planning to create a universal rating system that scores products based on how environmentally and socially sustainable they are, giving information on, for example, how much air pollution it created or how much water was used in its production. It is like a nutrition label, but for the environment.

Walmart will begin by asking each of its 100,000 suppliers around the world to answer fifteen questions about the sustainable practices of their enterprises. Questions include "Have you set publicly available greenhouse gas reduction targets? If yes, what are those targets?"[11] The proposal has won praise from many circles. "The beauty of the Walmart innovation," says professor and Walmart watcher Rosabeth Moss Kanter, "is that it doesn't ask anyone to change anything except the information that is provided and received. If polluters want to keep polluting, they are free to do so as long as they provide that data on their Walmart labels. And if consumers choose to buy from polluters whose labels they can read, they are free to do so."[12] In other words, Walmart is fixing an imperfection in the market. In a perfect market, consumers would have perfect information upon which to base their purchasing decisions. But while globalization has grown more complex and as environmental concerns have risen, the information available to customers has not kept pace. Walmart provides a reminder of how companies can step forward and address public issues that governments would not or have not addressed. Now for tens of thousands of companies and their millions of employees, environmental standards are a non-negotiable because working with Walmart is a nonnegotiable.

―――――

When Tom Stephens faced the fiberglass crisis, he was confronted with inconclusive evidence of a possible carcinogenic effect of fiberglass. The executive team worked intensely for weeks, meeting with legal, medical, and scientific experts. They considered every long-term option from doing nothing to exiting the fiberglass business entirely. But their immediate decision was clear—*inform*. Within hours of the symposium when Doll made the allegations about fiberglass, Manville posted warnings about the potential danger in every one of its facilities in the world.

Next, Stephens decided to pursue an aggressive relabeling campaign, to report the potential cancer risk to all their customers, distributors, and employees. The relabeling was not mandatory and the company's lawyers recommended against it, fearing that it could expose the company to unnecessary fear and even litigation. But Stephens and his team decided that those who were exposed to fiberglass had the right to make their own decisions about the risks. They believed that "the prosperity of a business is dependent upon being in step with the values of the society in which it operates" and that belief guided the team's actions. It paid off economically too. By executing the relabeling campaign openly, Manville won more business and increased goodwill from its customers.[13]

Each of the cases in this chapter exemplifies the challenges and opportunities leaders face in striving to create economic, social, and environmental prosperity. Manville had to do something, but both doing nothing and relabeling were risky. Manville's leaders had to rely on deeper values to guide them. Jacques Zwahlen faced a different, but significant risk when he learned about the conditions of child laborers in his supply chain. He protected his firm, but he did not stop there; he considered the second-order consequences of pulling out of the market completely, and as a result he began a program to take care of the children who would be affected. Walmart faced the least risk of the three scenarios, but the company is pushing forward with a strategy that puts a concern for environmental prosperity at the center. We live in a world of uncertainty. Manville could have relabeled fiberglass only to find itself punished by the market. At the moment of decision, no one can say what the outcomes will be. We can only act with our best knowledge and greatest courage.

The world is not what it ought to be. We do not have sustainable economic prosperity. Nine hundred twenty-three million people around the world live in slums, a number greater than the entire population of Europe. As of the time of this writing, 50 million people around the world are unemployed. We do not have sustainable social prosperity. Only one in six people globally can read or sign their name. According to the United Nations Working Group on Contemporary Forms of Slavery, an estimated 20 million people were held in bonded slavery during the last decade. We do not have sustainable environmental prosperity: 1.1 billion people in the world do not have access to safe, clean drinking water. Of the forty-two thousand deaths that occur every week from tainted water and a lack of basic sanitation, 90 percent are children under five years old.[14]

Although 99.9 percent of human DNA is the same from person to person, the differences among the way we live are stark. One-third of the world is well fed, one-third is underfed, and one-third is starving. In Japan, life expectancy is eighty-two years, but in Swaziland it is only thirty-two years.[15] It is as if we live on different planets. The seventh promise of the MBA Oath is recognition of this reality. It is an acknowledgment that we are not just an aggregation of atoms aimlessly bouncing off each other in space. We are knit together by our common humanity and ought to work together to make the world what it ought to be. It ought to be a world where no one is starving, where jobs are available for anyone willing to work hard, where preventable diseases are prevented, and where business leaders actually use their influence to address the biggest challenges facing their communities. We acknowledge businesses have different obligations than governments and nonprofits. In this pledge we are not saying that businesses should or can heal all the world's problems; we are saying that we should not be ignorant of the problems and should be aware of the ways we either contribute to the problems or contribute to their solutions. The world is not what it ought to be, but we can use our time, our skills, and our resources to make it better. As managers, we take seriously this opportunity and commit to connect our prosperity with the prosperity of all. We commit to engage in a partnership for living well.

13

ACCOUNTABILITY

I will be accountable to my peers and they will be accountable to me for living by this oath. I recognize that my stature and privileges as a professional stem from the respect and trust that the profession as a whole enjoys, and I accept my responsibility for embodying, protecting, and developing the standards of the management profession, so as to enhance that trust and respect.

MBA Oath, Eighth Promise

The MBA Oath stands for the better aspirations of business professionals. The challenge for us all now as oath signers is to make these aspirations real.

Ethan Cohen, Boston University, MBA 2009, signer #1704

O ne of the great stories of restoring trust through accountability is Warren Buffett's leadership of Salomon Brothers investment bank in the wake of a devastating scandal in 1991. In its heyday, Salomon Brothers was one of the hottest, highest-rolling bulge-bracket firms on Wall Street. Subject of the book *Liar's Poker,* Salomon specialized in mergers and proprietary trading. Salomon was founded in 1910 but hit its stride during the go-go '80s. It issued Wall Street's first

mortgage-backed security. After eighty years of operating, however, the storied bank ran into trouble.

In August of 1991, Salomon's government trading desk admitted
it had submitted unauthorized bids in the names of Salomon clients and had failed to disclose a commitment to buy U.S. Treasury
securities, enabling the bank to sidestep U.S. Treasury rules. This
was bad enough, but as investigators looked into the misdeeds, the
story was even worse. Eventually, the firm's top executives admitted
that they had known about the misconduct since April but had not
told the government. For nearly five months, the bank's leadership
deliberated without taking decisive action. Naturally, Salomon's
failure to disclose their discovery of the trades made people even
more curious. What other problems might also be hidden? The
bank's stock price tumbled from $36 to the mid-$20s.

It was a huge deal. Salomon had hidden wrongdoing instead
of punishing the perpetrators and correcting the situation.
Their brazenness was an affront to the U.S. Treasury. The revela-
tions sent shockwaves throughout the financial world, eventually
resulting in the resignations of President Thomas Strauss and
Solomon's legendary Chairman and CEO John Gutfreund.

Warren Buffett, the so-called Oracle of Omaha, was a Salomon
shareholder at the time. When Gutfreund resigned, Buffett was
elected chairman of the board. He immediately took action by out-
lining in a letter to investors the new principles of accountability
that he intended to use to guide the firm through this time of
trouble. Buffett spent $600,000 reprinting his third-quarter inves-
tor letter in the *Wall Street Journal*, the *Financial Times*, the *New York
Times*, and the *Washington Post*. Buffett described his conviction that
a profitable business could be built on strong principles. "Salomon
has the capacity amid favorable market conditions to earn substantial sums." Using a metaphor from tennis, he said, "I believe we can

earn these superior returns playing aggressively in the center of the court, without resorting to close-to-the-line acrobatics. Good profits simply are not inconsistent with good behavior. Our goal is going to be that stated many decades ago by J. P. Morgan, who wished to see his bank transact 'first-class business . . . in a first-class way.' We will judge ourselves in fact not only by the business we do, but also by the business we decline to do."[1]

In the letter he demanded that each of Salomon's employees "be guided by a test that goes beyond rules: contemplating any business act, an employee should ask himself whether he would be willing to see it immediately described by an informed and critical reporter on the front page of his local paper, there to be read by his spouse, children and friends. At Salomon we simply want no part of any activities that pass legal tests but that we, as citizens, would find offensive." Buffett's letter advocated for the spirit of the law, for doing business ethically, and for sustainable economic prosperity, and it demonstrated why Buffett had earned the nickname "Mr. Integrity."

―――――

The MBA Oath's final promise is simple: "I will be accountable to my peers and they will be accountable to me for living by this oath." Accountability is the acknowledgment of a duty and an assumption of responsibility. If you are taking an oath, you should be expected to live by the promises you make. But this final pledge underscores the seriousness of taking the oath in the first place. You are saying: *Hold me to this. Don't let me off the hook. And I won't let you off the hook either.*

In our view, accountability is premised on the idea that peer-enforced norms are a better route to responsible action than are legal obligations. Regulation creates loopholes; personal motivation with peer accountability creates a stronger ethos for conduct. Accountability means oath signers anticipate potential affronts to ethical behavior and rely on their community to help navigate decisions. This self-monitoring approach to business conduct is the best way to regain society's trust in the worthy profession of management.

Buffett did not promise that Salomon would be perfect and free from mistakes. "As is the case at all large organizations, there will be mistakes at Salomon and even failures, but to the best of our ability we will acknowledge our errors quickly and correct them with equal promptness." However, he would have zero tolerance for any legal violation or moral failure. He wrote that if his traders and deal makers lost money for the firm, he would be understanding, but if they lost "a shred of reputation," he would be "ruthless." He demanded that any employee found in violation be reported "instantaneously and directly to me." He even gave his home phone number and instructed employees to call him if they saw something funny.

Did Warren Buffett really need to give out his home phone number? No, maybe not. But the symbolic importance of the act is unmistakable: *I am willing to do whatever it takes to win back our shareholders' trust in this company.* That is what being accountable is about. *I am going to do what it takes to honor my word and you can hold me to it.* It is actions like these that have made Buffett the gold standard for business accountability.

It is Saturday. We are in a Barnes & Noble in Manhattan, sitting in the café, trying to write, but utterly failing because we are so distracted by what is happening twelve feet away. A young kid, probably in high school, is sitting at a table with his father. We guess they are from out of town because they have a stack of seven New York City guidebooks piled up in front of them. What catches our attention is not that they are obviously tourists. What grabs our attention is that the father, who is hurriedly reviewing the guidebooks, pauses now and then and passes the book to his son, who spreads the book open on the table and takes a surreptitious photo of the page with his digital camera. The barista behind the bar does not notice the activity, and when her attention finally returns to the tables, the father gestures to his son. They close the books, leave them on the table, stand up, and amble out the door. The sights and sounds of New York City await them, and the images on their camera will be their guide.

Our generation came of age at a time like no other. We grew up in a world where songs and movies can be downloaded on a computer without paying for them; and digital photos can be captured from books without buying the books. Who knows, you may be sitting in a bookstore taking photos of the pages of this book at this moment. If so, we assure you we are flattered. But please stop.

Should we have said something? Should the other customers have? Where was the accountability in the bookstore? Where is the accountability for the MBA Oath? There are two questions of accountability related to the MBA Oath. First, how will we *make ourselves* accountable to living out our principles? Second, how can we *hold each other* accountable?

How Will We Make Ourselves Accountable?

From the beginning, we made accountability central to the MBA Oath. First, we decided to have our class take the oath together publicly. We stood together, shoulder to shoulder, and recited the words of the oath as a commitment to each other. When we got to the line about being held accountable, we watched as people around the room looked at each other and let the weight of the promise sink in.

Second, everyone, from our very first signer to our most recent, has had to add his or her name to our public roll online at www.mbaoath.org. By making the commitment public and lasting online, we feel the oath will be taken more seriously. For as long as the site is online, the person who has taken the MBA Oath has a public commitment to stand by the promises he or she made. This may sound like too simple a tool for accountability, but there are many other examples where just putting the information online leads to increased accountability.

Congressional representatives are more accountable for their voting records now that both their voting records and political contributions are online. Service contractors (e.g., plumbers, electricians, etc.) are more accountable because users can now read reviews online. Recently, two private equity executives took it upon themselves to fight white-collar crime by adding to the punishment doled out by the courts. Prison terms are not enough, they reasoned. The biggest con artists need to have their names in lights in perpetuity. So they launched a Web site, http://www.thehallofinfamy.org, designed as an educational tool to help readers understand and prevent white-collar crime. The site features profiles of the biggest fraudsters and con artists of all time.

Dean Karlan, a Yale behavioral economist, takes online accountability a step further. He has founded a Web site, www .stickk.com, that allows users to make financial commitments as a motivation to achieve a goal by a certain date. The person puts up money by credit card and creates a challenge for himself (stop smoking, lose ten pounds, etc.) and a way to verify that he met the goal (weigh in at a doctor's clinic). If he meets his goal, he gets his money back. If he fails to meet his goal, the money goes to charity. We do not know if a similar system would work to hold members of a profession accountable to professional standards, but we are confident that in the coming years more creative people will find ways to apply new Web technologies, from Twitter to Facebook, to help increase accountability.

How Will We Keep Each Other Accountable?

We have no doubt that some have taken the oath whose lives may not be the paradigm of wisdom and ethical sense. Nevertheless, they took the oath and find themselves in the company of people who have sworn to live and abide by certain principles. By identifying with that group publicly, the impetus to change negative patterns of behavior is likely improved. Being a member of that group is certainly not going to serve as any inducement to further negative behavior. The reason Alcoholics Anonymous is the most effective program devised for reforming alcoholics is that it utilizes the power of the group to heal and bring about reconciliation of the alcoholic with his own self, a Higher Power, and the community as a whole. Isolation is the context in which many people make unfortunate life choices.

Already, as of the time of this writing, we are working to create more tools to help people meet their commitments and to hold them accountable for their failure to do so. Two simple ideas we are working with are a time capsule e-mail and lifeline. The time capsule e-mail springs from the idea that everyone needs to be reminded occasionally of what he or she values. We could encourage all signers of the oath to log on to our Web site and write an e-mail to themselves about why they are signing the MBA Oath and what it means to them. Then we would e-mail those letters back to their respective authors every year. The letters would serve as an ongoing reminder and accountability tool for the signers to keep the oath.

We are also thinking of asking all signers to designate a "lifeline" whom they can call when they get into a jam. On the television game show *Who Wants to Be a Millionaire?* contestants are given the chance to call their lifeline, a previously selected friend with good trivia knowledge, when they do not know the answer to a question. If the lifeline is good, she can help the person determine the correct answer to the question and move a step closer to winning the game. The same concept would apply with a professional lifeline. We may at some time find ourselves in a professional situation in which we do not know what to do. We ought to have a friend who shares the same values whom we can call when that time comes. In those difficult hours, we need at least one person to whom we can turn for the right, if difficult advice.

So what if you are the lifeline? Earlier we talked about the concept of dieting. You are far more likely to succeed in your diet if you tell your friends about it than if you keep it to yourself. But what if you are not the dieter but the dieter's friend? What is your responsibility? How involved do you get? The answer depends on the answer to another question: How much do you care? If you care enough, your answer is simple—you will do whatever it takes.

In some marriage ceremonies, the officiant will address the gathered congregation after administering the vows between the bride and groom. He will ask whether the gathered witnesses will do all in their power to strengthen and uphold the newly wedded couple. The role of the wedding party is to stand by the couple during the ceremony, to give a physical symbol of the friends' commitment to the couple to be there for them. In the same way, every signer of the oath is pledging to stand by every other signer, to hold each one of them accountable, to spur them on. This is as it should be. We should be a community of leaders who together are seeking to be our best selves and lead with true integrity and character.

———

The MBA Oath is a progressive step toward the goal of professional accountability. A student at Oxford's Said Business School wrote the following online: "Many of us have found this initiative to resonate with our own convictions. The point of an MBA should not just be about equipping individuals with tools for their own enrichment, but also to deepen our appreciation about the impact of our actions."[2] But what specific actions can signers take when faced with an ethical dilemma? We need to ask ourselves hard questions whose answers will guide our decision making. These are the tests of visibility, generality, and legacy.

Warren Buffett put forth the visibility test, or the so-called *Wall Street Journal* test, in his letter to Salomon shareholders: Would I be comfortable if this action were described on the front page of a respected newspaper? What if your mother opened up the newspaper to see your name in an unflattering light? Would you be comfortable with that?

The generality test is an application of the Golden Rule: Would I be comfortable if everyone in a similar situation did this? If everyone in my organization took this route, would our reputation and viability remain intact?

The legacy test is about your future. Is this how I'd like my leadership legacy to be remembered?

If you can answer yes to all three of these questions, then you should feel comfortable with your plan of action

There is a section of Homer's *Odyssey* that tells of Odysseus sailing by the isle of the sirens. The sirens were known for their enchanting songs, sung from the cliffs of their island. So strong and compelling was their singing that sailors frequently shipwrecked upon the rocks of the island because they were so inescapably drawn to the sound. Odysseus knew of the temptation, so he had himself lashed to the mast of the ship, and had all of the sailors fill their ears with beeswax as they went past the island. Odysseus commanded them not to untie him, no matter what he said, because he would go temporarily insane. Not until their ship had passed well safe of the island did the sailors let Odysseus go, and they were safe.

That is the picture of accountability: both being accountable and being held accountable. It is not relying on your own strength. It is admitting your weakness and asking for help. It is confessing, "I am going to be tempted by the sirens' song so badly that you need to tie me to the mast." It is giving permission to the people on your crew to hold you to your word. Just as Odysseus had to admit his need for accountability, the sailors needed to do the hard work of holding him accountable. They had to tie the man down and ignore his screams and pleas as they passed by the island. Odysseus probably hated them in the moment and cursed them for their lack of sympathy. But the sailors held him accountable. And they all survived.

Nothing else in the oath matters if we do not keep this eighth and final promise. It does not matter what we say if our actions do not match our words. We can promise to be saints. We can promise to be angels. We can promise anything we like, but none of it matters if we are not accountable for it. Therefore, let us not wait for law, regulation, or other enforcement to move us to positive action. As MBAs, we should exercise the muscles of self-monitoring to raise a standard and develop our profession.

In chapter 4, we discussed how there are some who say that unless we kick people off the list of signers for violations of the oath, then we have no accountability at all. It may be true. A code of conduct may only work if a professional body monitors behavior and withdraws credentials for violations. That is how it works in the fields of medicine, engineering, and law. Long before there were national councils to do this monitoring, there were local groups, tied to universities who did it.

That might be the next step for the MBA degree. Each school could set for its own graduates standards that are broadly in alignment with the principles of the MBA Oath. That might be the only way to add some real stick. Or perhaps, a broad cross-school consensus on enforcement will emerge. It is unlikely that management will become a licensed profession with licenses that can be revoked. But even today the alumni status of MBAs is very valuable. An affiliation with a school is an important source of business networking and a stamp of approval on a résumé. If alumni knew their status were at risk should they violate the principles of the profession, they might think twice before fleecing their investors or lying to their boards.

Even that is likely years from fruition. In the meantime, we are taking steps forward. We are proposing a general set of principles to work by. We are contemplating and constructing the institutional infrastructure to support them. The important things at this juncture are the ideas and the willingness to be held accountable to them.

It has been said of the people of ancient Athens that when the freedom they wished for most was freedom from responsibility, they ceased to be free and were never free again. In our times, too many for too long have wished to be free of responsibility. We say no. Let us take on responsibility. Our ultimate ability to operate our enterprises in a free society is worth the weight of responsibility that comes with that liberty.

EPILOGUE

We must decide what our era stands for. Let's bring the basic principles of life—responsibility, accountability, fairness, and honesty—to everything we, management professionals, do. Let's put business to good use and use business to bring about good in the world.

—*Umaimah Mendhro, Harvard, Class of 2009, signer #12*

The world has changed. In the aftermath of the 2008 economic collapse, the federal government became the largest shareholder of our country's largest automaker, largest insurance company, and largest bank. A new age has dawned, and we are just beginning to learn how to deal with it. Our generation is beginning their careers in the midst of the worst economy since the Great Depression. The stock market continues its rise and fall—with arguments over a single-dip versus double-dip recovery. Unemployment is encroaching on double-digit territory. At the time of this writing, over ten million people have lost their jobs. Business schools are challenged with cries of "irrelevance." The *Economist* is now publishing articles about the end of the public's love affair with MBAs.

It is not just MBAs who are in trouble. Capitalism itself is at risk. James Q. Wilson, a professor of management at UCLA, has argued that capitalists should recognize "that while free markets will ruthlessly eliminate inefficient firms, the moral sentiments of man will only gradually and uncertainly penalize immoral ones. But, while the quick destruction of inefficient corporations threatens only individual firms, the slow anger at immoral ones threatens capitalism, and thus freedom itself."[1] We are seeing it already.

The time to act with fire, determination, and unbending commitment is now. The MBA Oath continues on—both as a movement and an organization. What was initially a movement in one school by one class of students has grown to embody thousands of MBA students and alumni across hundreds of schools and many classes of graduates. The real work is just beginning.

The MBA Oath is now a formal organization with a mission to create a movement around the principles embodied by the oath. The class of 2010 is building on the work we began. MBA students at Babson and Baltimore, Harvard and Yale, Kellogg and Columbia are coming together to discuss how to make the MBA Oath come alive on campus. The University of Strathclyde, in Glasgow, Scotland, became our first student-led initiative in the United Kingdom. We held a leadership summit for current MBA students in New York City. We knew the MBA Oath had a unifying effect when both Duke and Carolina students sat together in active collaboration to discuss the MBA Oath on the brink of basketball season.

Elsewhere, the Young Global Leaders group at the World Economic Forum progresses toward the admirable goal of a global oath for managers. We share their enthusiasm for a vision that involves businesspeople—MBA or otherwise—standing shoulder to shoulder across geographic boundaries, firmly planted on a common set of convictions. A shift in the business paradigm is not limited to MBAs, nor can it be made by MBAs alone.

Much work is yet to be done. We will not change the world with a roll call of signers alone. We call upon current MBA students, MBA graduates, academics, and all other business practitioners, regardless of whether they are MBA graduates, to work together to make management a profession and set higher standards for business.

It is worth reflecting on whether our goal is living "the good life" or living a great life. Both kinds of lives compete for our attention. On the one hand, we want to live a great life, to make a difference, to leave our mark. We want to build things. We want to leave our footprints in the sand. We want to be remembered for having contributed something of significance and value to the world. On the other hand, we also dream of the good life, a successful life, a safe life. We want a life of wealth, comfort, and convenience, one where we avoid suffering and we get what we want. Neither the dream of the good life nor dream of the great life is wrong. But they are dreams that at times may be at odds with each other. To the extent you avoid suffering in the short-term, you may be compromising your long-term ability to make a difference. The unalterable fact is living by the oath may require sacrifice.

Look at almost any list of people's heroes and you will see the contest between greatness and comfort is often a zero-sum game. Lincoln, Gandhi, Martin Luther King Jr. each lived heroically, but they lost their lives as a result. No image of "the good life" would include working shoeless and in poverty among the lepers of Calcutta, or enduring twenty-seven years of imprisonment in South Africa. Yet we must agree that Mother Teresa and Nelson Mandela lived lives of incomparable greatness for these very reasons. As James M. Barrie wrote, you can have anything in life if you will sacrifice everything else for it. The question is, What do want? How small or how big is your vision?

John F. Kennedy once said, "Do not pray for easy lives. Pray to be stronger men. Do not pray for tasks equal to your powers. Pray for power equal to your tasks." Our exhortation is not for everyone to join a nonprofit or to abandon life paths that may lead to riches. Our point is that wherever you are—whether it be Wall Street or Washington, Mozambique or Morgan Stanley—you work not just for the small dream of advancing yourself but also for the larger dream of making the world a better place.

We can do anything with either great nobility or great meanness. We can exalt humble careers by the way we conduct ourselves, or we can lay low exalted careers by our own venality. The choice is ours, and it is liberating. Martin Luther King Jr. said, "If you are called to be a street sweeper, sweep streets even as Michelangelo painted, or Beethoven composed music, or Shakespeare wrote poetry. Sweep streets so well that all the hosts of heaven and earth will pause to say, 'Here lived a great street sweeper who did his job well.'"

The world looks to business for leadership. What kind of leaders will we be? Let us be leaders with dignity, who refuse to collude in our own defeat, who refuse to put our job security above our honor, who prize our character even more highly than our cash flow statements. Let us be the ones who stand in the gap after the earthquake and repair the damage. Let us be men and women who live out the meaning of the MBA Oath, people who are defined not by extracting value but by creating it; people who are known for their integrity, their ethics, and their visionary leadership.

Notes

INTRODUCTION

1. Philip Delves Broughton, "Harvard's Masters of the Apocalypse," *Sunday Times* (London), March 1, 2009, http://www.timesonline.co.uk/tol/news/uk/education/article5821706.ece.

2. Matt Lynn, "The MBA Scam . . . " *mattlynn.blogspot.com*, July 23, 2009, http://mattlynn.blogspot.com/2009/07/mba-scam.html.

3. Paul Steinhauser, "Poll: Politicians Trusted More Than Business on the Economy," *CNNPolitics.com*, February 23, 2009, www.cnn.com/2009/POLITICS/02/.../poll.economy/index.html.

4. Elana Berkowitz, "Business Graduates: Do No Harm," *Guardian*, June 17, 2009, http://www.guardian.co.uk/commentisfree/cifamerica/2009/jun/17/harvard-mba-oath-business-ethics.

5. Shoshana Zuboff, "The Old Solutions Have Become the New Problems," *BusinessWeek*, July 2, 2009, http://www.businessweek.com/managing/content/jul2009/ca2009072_489734.htm.

6. Richard Edelman, "The MBA Oath," *www.edelman.com/speak_up/blog*, June 5, 2009, http://www.edelman.com/speak_up/blog/archives/2009/06/the_mba_oath.html.

7. David Gergen, "How Business Can Stand Tall Again," *Fortune*, May 4, 2009, http://money.cnn.com/2009/05/04/news/economy/gergen_business.fortune/index.htm.

8. Description partially based on a Harvard Business School Case Study. Wendy K. Smith and Richard S. Tedlow, "James Burke, A Career in American Business (A)," April 20, 1989, prod. #: 389177-PDF-ENG (Boston: Harvard Business Publishing).

9. Peter Drucker in *The Heart of a Business Ethic* (Lanham, MD: University Press of America, 2005), 55.

CHAPTER 1: THE TROUBLE WITH BUSINESS SCHOOLS

1. This "works" in a situation like the past few years where 40 to 50 percent of MBA graduates go to work in financial services where the compensation packages tend to be high. It remains to be seen what will happen when employment opportunities dry up as a result of the financial crisis or if Washington changes the rules of executive compensation.
2. Proposed fixes from Joel Podolny, "The Buck Stops (and Starts) at Business School," *Harvard Business Review*, June 1, 2009: 66–67.
3. John Terrill, Director of the Center for Integrity in Business at Seattle Pacific University, "Reframing Business Education," *http://apprenticeplace.wordpress.com*, June 24, 2009, http://apprenticeplace.wordpress.com/2009/06/24/reframing-business-education/.
4. Joel Podolny, "The Buck Stops (and Starts) at Business School," 66–67.
5. Barry Mitnick, "The Case Against the Case Method," *blogs.harvardbusiness.org*, April 29, 2009, http://blogs.harvardbusiness.org/how-to-fix-business-schools/2009/04/the-case-against-the-case-meth-1.html.
6. Robert F. Bruner, "I, a New M.B.A., Solemnly Swear," *Forbes*, June 8, 2009, http://www.forbes.com/2009/06/08/business-school-mba-opinions-contributors-oath-of-honor.html.

CHAPTER 2: THE GREAT, BUT DELICATE EXPERIMENT

1. Owen D. Young. "Dedication Address," in *Dedication Addresses*, a compilation of transcripts of speeches and related documents from the dedication of the Harvard Business School campus on June 4, 1927, reprinted from the July 1927 issue of *Harvard Business Review* and now in the HBS Archives Collection (AC 1927 17.1), 6–7.
2. Quotes taken from business school Web sites.
3. Melvin T. Copeland, *And Mark an Era: The Story of the Harvard Business School* (Boston: Little, Brown, 1958), 119–20.

4. Roger Thompson, "Harvard Business School Discusses Future of the MBA," *Harvard Business School Working Knowledge*, November 24, 2008, http://hbswk.hbs.edu/item/6053.html. See also Rakesh Khurana, *From Higher Aims to Hired Hands: The Social Transformation of American Business Schools and the Unfulfilled Promise of Management as a Profession* (Princeton, NJ: Princeton University Press, 2007).

5. Angel Cabrera, "Let's Professionalize Management," *Harvard Business School Press Blog*, April 27, 2009, http://blogs.harvardbusiness.org/how-to-fix-business-schools/2009/04/a-hippocratic-oath-for-future.html.

6. Joel Podolny, "The Buck Stops (and Starts) at Business School," *Harvard Business Review*, June 1, 2009: 66–67.

7. Rakesh Khurana and Nitin Nohria, "Management Needs to Become a Profession," *Financial Times*, October 20, 2008, http://www.ft.com.

CHAPTER 3: A HIPPOCRATIC OATH FOR BUSINESS

1. Fareed Zakaria, "The Capitalist Manifesto: Greed Is Good (To a Point)," *Newsweek*, June 13, 2009, http://www.newsweek.com/id/201935.

2. Ibid.

3. Ibid.

4. Charles Handy, "What Is a Business For?" *Harvard Business Review*, December 1, 2002.

5. Rakesh Khurana and Nitin Nohria, "It's Time to Make Management a True Profession," *Harvard Business Review*, October 1, 2008: 1.

6. Example drawn from class notes in Leadership and Corporate Accountability.

CHAPTER 4: SIX MORE ARGUMENTS FOR THE MBA OATH

1. Dana Mattioli, "Professor Says Business Schools and Students Can Take Away Lessons From Financial Crisis," *Wall Street Journal*, August 20, 2009.

2. Our thoughts on the two risks investors face are partly influenced by Howard Marks in "So Much That's False and Nutty," Oaktree Capital investor newsletter, http://oaktreecapital.com, July 2009.

3. Al Sikes, "On Forswearing Greed," Provocations blog post, July 24, 2009, http://www.ttf.org/index/journal/detail/forswearing-greed/.

4. Executive Briefing, *The Millennium Poll on Corporate Social Responsibility,* conducted by Environics International, Ltd., in cooperation with The Prince of Wales Business Leaders Forum and The Conference Board, 1999, http://www.environics.net/eil/milennium/.

5. Aleksandr Solzhenitsyn, Harvard University Class Day Address, June 8, 1978, http://www.columbia.edu/cu/augustine/arch/solzhenitsyn/harvard1978.html.

CHAPTER 5: THE PURPOSE OF A MANAGER

1. Tom Chappell, *The Soul of a Business* (New York: Bantam, 1993), 62.

2. Peter Singer, "Can Business Be Ethical?" *Project Syndicate, 2009,* http://www.independent.com.mt/news.asp?newsitemid=89667 (accessed January 8, 2010).

3. From the Johnson & Johnson corporate Web site, http://www.jnj.com/connect/about-jnj/jnj-credo/.

4. As quoted in Michael Novak, *Business as a Calling* (New York: Free Press, 1996), 141.

5. *Dodge Brothers v. Ford Motor Company.* 170 N.W. 668 (Mich. 1919).

6. Allan Nevins and Frank E. Hill, *Ford: Expansion and Challenge 1915–1933* (New York: Scribner, 1957).

7. William T. Allen, "Our Schizophrenic Conception of the Business Corporation," *Cardozo Law Review* 14, no. 2 (1992): 2, 5.

8. Michael Novak, *Business as a Calling*, 141.

9. William T. Allen, "Our Schizophrenic Conception of the Business Corporation," 7–8.

10. Donald Soderquist, "The Integration of Faith in the Workplace," in *The Heart of a Business Ethic,* ed. William C. Pollard (Lanham, MD: University Press of America, 2005), 184.

11. Charles Handy, "What Is a Business For?" *Harvard Business Review,* December 1, 2002: 5.

12. Howard Marks, "So Much That's False and Nutty," Oaktree Capital investor newsletter, http://oaktreecapital.com, July 2009.

13. Angel Cabrera, "Let's Professionalize Management," *Harvard Business Review Blog Debate: How to Fix Business School,* April 27, 2009, http://blogs .hbr.org/how-to-fix-business-schools/2009/04/a-hippocratic-oath-for-future.html.

CHAPTER 6: ETHICS AND INTEGRITY

1. Donald Soderquist, "The Integration of Faith in the Workplace," in *The Heart of a Business Ethic,* ed. William C. Pollard (Lanham, MD: University Press of America, 2005), 181.

2. Immanuel Kant, *Grounding for the Metaphysics of Morals,* 3rd ed., trans. James W. Ellington (Indianapolis, IN: Hackett, 1993), 30.

3. Based on surveys in Vancouver and Toronto, 1984–85. From Kahneman, Knesch, Thaler, "Fairness as a Constraint on Profit Seeking: Entitlements in the Market," *American Economic Review,* September 1986.

4. Donald McCabe, "MBAs Cheat, But Why?" *Harvard Business Review Blog Debate: How to Fix Business Schools,* April 13, 2009, http://blogs.harvard business.org/how-to-fix-business-schools/2009/04/mbas-cheat-but-why .html.

5. Aine Donovon, "Can Ethics Classes Cure Cheating?" *Harvard Business Review Blog Debate: How to Fix Business Schools,* April 14, 2009, http://blogs .hbr.org/how-to-fix-business-schools/2009/04/can-ethics-classes-cure-cheating.html.

6. Dan Ariely, "How Honest People Cheat," *Harvard Business Review,* January 29, 2008, http://blogs.harvardbusiness.org/cs/2008/01/how_honest_people_ cheat.html.

7. Ibid.

8. Dan Heath and Chip Heath, "In Defense of Feelings," *Fast Company,* July–August 2009: 58.

9. Jane Hamilton, *A Map of the World* (New York: First Anchor Books Edition, 1995).

10. Donald Soderquist, "The Integration of Faith in the Workplace," 187.

11. Stanley Milgram, "The Perils of Obedience," *Harper's,* December 1963: 62.

12. Aleksandr Solzhenitsyn, *The Gulag Archipeligo 1919–1956* (New York: Harper Collins, 2002), 312.

13. "Why Good People Do Bad Things," *Harvard Business Review*, June 9, 2009: 59.

CHAPTER 7: NO MAN IS AN ISLAND

1. We studied the case of Malden Mills while at business school. For the complete case, contact Harvard Business School Publishing. Nitin Nohria, Thomas R. Piper, and Bridget Gurtler, "Malden Mills (A)," December 10, 2003, prod. #: 404072-PDF-ENG.

2. Bruce Butterfield, "Test by Fire: The Story of Malden Mills, Pt. 2," *Boston Globe*, September 8, 1996: 7.

3. Rebecca Leung, "The Mensch of Malden Mills," *60 Minutes*, CBS, July 6, 2009, http://www.cbsnews.com/stories/2003/07/03/60minutes/main561656.shtml.

4. Michael Arndt, "How O'Neill Got Alcoa Shining," *BusinessWeek*, February 12, 2001, http://www.businessweek.com/2001/01_06/b3718006.htm.

5. Dan Heath and Chip Heath, "Why Your Gut Is More Ethical Than Your Brain," *Fast Company*, July 1, 2009, http://www.fastcompany.com/magazine/137/made-to-stick-in-defense-of-feelings.html.

6. Michael Arndt, "How O'Neill Got Alcoa Shining."

7. Jay Goltz, "Business Ethics and Serving the Greater Good," You're the Boss blog, *New York Times*, June 26, 2009, http://boss.blogs.nytimes.com/2009/06/26/business-ethics-and-serving-the-greater-good/.

8. Ibid.

9. E. Allan Lind, Jerald Greenberg, Kimberly S. Scott, and Thomas D. Welchans, "The Winding Road from Employee to Complainant: Situational and Psychological Determinants of Wrongful-Termination Claims," *Administrative Science Quarterly* 45 (2000): 557–590.

10. Fritidsresor description loosely based on a Harvard Business School Case Study. Joshua D. Margolis, Vincent Dessain, and Anders Sjoman, "Fritidsresor Under Pressure (A): The First 10 Hours," September 17, 2006, prod. #: 407007-PDF-ENG (Boston: Harvard Business Publishing).

11. Adapted from T. L. Beauchamp and J. F. Childress, *Principles of Biomedical Ethics* (New York: Oxford University Press, 2001), 115.

12. Class notes from our Leadership and Corporate Accountability course, Harvard Business School.

CHAPTER 8: AMBITION AND GOOD FAITH

1. This story is based on the Harvard Business School Case Study "Parable of the Sadhu" by Bowen McCoy, May 1, 1997, prod. #: 97307-PDF-ENG (Boston: Harvard Business Publishing).

2. Adam Smith in *The Wealth of Nations*, 5th ed. (London: Methuen & Co. Ltd, 1904), I.2.2.

3. *Wall Street*, DVD, directed by Oliver Stone (1987; 20th Century Fox, 20th Anniversary DVD, 2007).

4. John M. Darley and C. Daniel Batson, "From Jerusalem to Jericho: A Study of Situational and Dispositional Variables in Helping Behavior," *Journal of Personality and Social Psychology* 27, no. 100 (1973).

5. Bowen McCoy, "Parable of the Sadhu."

6. Kathleen D. Vohs, Nicole L. Mead, and Miranda R. Goode, "The Psychological Consequences of Money," *Science* 314 (November 17, 2006).

7. "The Giant Pool of Money," *This American Life*, hosted by Ira Glass, National Public Radio, episode 355, May 29, 2008, http://www.thisamericanlife .org/Radio_Episode.aspx?episode=355.

8. Ibid.

9. Ibid.

10. Dan Heath and Chip Heath, "In Defense of Feelings," *Fast Company*, July–August 2009: 58.

11. David Young, "The Nature of the Exercise of Authority," in *The Heart of a Business Ethic*, ed. William C. Pollard (Lanham, MD: University Press of America, 2005), 181.

12. "A Hippocratic oath to heal the business world, but is there a cure for human greed?" *Business Day South Africa*, June 15, 2009, http://www .businessday.co.za/articles/Content.aspx?id=73403.

13. Bowen McCoy, "Parable of the Sadhu."

14. Model Business Corporation Act, Section 8.30(a), http://www.abanet .org/buslaw/library/onlinepublications/mbca2002.pdf. Also Committee on Corporate Laws, *The Corporate Director's Guidebook*, 5th ed. (Chicago: American Bar Association, Section of Business Law, 2007).

15. *Meinhard v. Salmon* 249 N.Y. 458; 164 N.E. 545 (1928).

CHAPTER 9: THE LETTER AND THE SPIRIT OF THE LAW

1. World Development Indicators Database, http://www.nationmaster.com/graph/gov_tim_req_to_sta_a_bus_day-time-required-start-business-days.

2. John Marty, " 'Costly' Government Regulations Shown to Yield Big Returns," in *To the Point!*, December 4, 2003, http://www.apple-pie.org/ttp/default.asp?articleid=42.

3. Ibid.

4. Ibid.

5. Brian Griffiths, "The Business of Values," in *The Heart of a Business Ethic*, ed. William C. Pollard (Lanham, MD: University Press of America, 2005), 36.

6. Professor Rohit Deshpande and Research Associate Lara Winig, "Cipla," Harvard Business School Case Study, rev. May 10, 2006, prod. #: 9-503-085 (Boston: Harvard Business Publishing), 7.

7. "India's Cipla Dismisses Glaxo 'Piracy' Allegation," Reuters, March 13, 2001.

8. Scott Schaefer, "MBA Oath," *Utah Economist*, July 22, 2009, http://utah-economist.blogspot.com/2009/07/mba-oath-continued_22.html.

CHAPTER 10: RESPONSIBILITY AND TRANSPARENCY

1. Story based on the Harvard Business School Case Study "Beech-Nut Nutrition Corporation (A)" by Lynn S. Paine, November 29, 2003, prod. #: 392084-PDF-ENG (Boston: Harvard Business Publishing).

2. Michael C. Jensen, "A New Model of Integrity: An Actionable Pathway to Trust, Productivity and Value" (presentation, INSEAD Social Innovation Research Seminar Series, Fontainebleu, France, March 16, 2009).

3. Ibid.

4. Ibid.

5. Charles Kindleberger, *Manias, Panics, and Crashes,* 5th ed. (Hoboken, NJ: Wiley, 2005), 167.

6. Albert Z. Carr, "Is Business Bluffing Ethical," *Harvard Business Review* (January 1,1968): 143–153.

7. Ibid.

8. Charles Kindleberger, *Manias, Panics, and Crashes,* 177–8.

9. Alexei Barrionuevo, "Questioning the Books," *Wall Street Journal,* February 26, 2002.

10. James O'Toole and Warren Bennis, "What's Needed Next: A Culture of Candor," *Harvard Business Review,* June 1, 2009: 56.

11. Ibid.

12. Ibid.

13. Martin Luther King Jr., Letter from a Birmingham Jail, April 16, 1963, http://mlk-kpp01.stanford.edu/index.php/resources/article/annotated_letter_from_birmingham/.

CHAPTER 11: PERSONAL AND PROFESSIONAL GROWTH

1. John Gardner, "Personal Renewal," speech, McKinsey & Company, Phoenix, Arizona, November 10 1990, http://www.pbs.org/johngardner/sections/writings_speech_1.html.

2. Ibid.

3. Stephen R. Covey, *The 7 Habits of Highly Effective People* (New York: Fireside, 1989), 287.

4. David Whyte, *Crossing the Unknown Sea: Work as a Pilgrimage of Identity* (New York: Riverhead, 2002), 3.

5. Scott Snook, "Leader(ship) Development," Harvard Business School Case Study, October 4, 2007, prod. #: 9-408-064 (Boston: Harvard Business Publishing), 12–13.

6. M. W. McCall Jr., *High Flyers* (Boston: Harvard Business Publishing, 1998), inside flap.

7. Bill George and Peter Sims, *True North: Discover Your Authentic Leadership* (San Francisco: Wiley, 2007), xxxiii–xxxiv.

8. David A. Garvin, personal communication, March 2009.

9. David A. Garvin, *Learning in Action* (Boston: Harvard Business Publishing, 2000), chapter 1.

10. Ibid.

11. Ibid.

12. Steve Kerr, "Don't Blame the Business Schools," *Harvard Business Review,* April 2, 2009, http://blogs.hbr.org/how-to-fix-business-schools/2009/04/dont-blame-the-business-school.html.

13. Alan Greenspan, "The Fed Didn't Cause the Housing Bubble," *Wall Street Journal,* March 11, 2009: A15.

CHAPTER 12: SUSTAINING PROSPERITY AND LIVING WELL

1. Stephen W. Quickel, "Triumph of Wile," *Business Month,* November 1988: 30.

2. Lynn Sharp Paine and Research Associate Sarah B. Grant, "Manville Corporation Fiber Glass Group (A)," Harvard Business School Case Study, prod. #: 9-394-117 (Boston: Harvard Business Publishing, 1993), 11.

3. Tom Morris, *If Aristotle Ran General Motors* (New York: Holt, 1996), 102, 104.

4. Ibid.

5. M. Satchell, *U.S. News & World Report,* June 25, 1990: 27.

6. Fareed Zakaria, *The Post-American World* (New York: Norton, 2008), 89–90.

7. Bruce Einhorn, "Chinese Get Angrier About Pollution," *BusinessWeek,* September 2, 2009, http://www.businessweek.com/globalbiz/content/sep2009/gb2009092_230895.htm.

8. Howard Marks, "So Much That's False and Nutty." Oaktree Capital investor newsletter, http://oaktreecapital.com, July 2009.

9. Lynn Sharp Paine, *Value Shift* (New York: McGraw-Hill, 2003), 235–236.

10. Response by Lynn Sharp Paine, in *The Heart of a Business Ethic,* ed. Donald Holt (Lanham, MD: University Press of America, 2005), 94–95.

11. Stephanie Rosenbloom, "At Wal-Mart, Labeling to Reflect Green Intent," *New York Times,* July 15, 2009, http://www.nytimes.com/2009/07/16/business/energy-environment/16walmart.html.

12. Rosabeth Moss Kanter, "Wal-Mart's Environmental Game-Changer," July 16, 2009, http://blogs.harvardbusiness.org/kanter/2009/07/walmarts-environmental-gamecha.html?cm_mmc=npv-_-TOPICEMAIL-_-JUL_2009-_-INNOVATION2.

13. Lynn Sharp Paine, *Value Shift*, 235.

14. Data from Charity Water, http://www.charitywater.org/whywater/.

15. CIA World Fact Book, https://www.cia.gov/library/publications/the-world-factbook/rankorder/2102rank.html. Accessed January 20, 2010.

CHAPTER 13: ACCOUNTABILITY

1. Source material from: Lynne Sharp Paine and Michael Santoro. "Salomon Brothers (A)," Harvard Business School Case Study, prod. #: 9-305-019 (Boston: Harvard Business Publishing, 2005).

2. Nic Paton, "The MBA Oath: A New Era of Responsibility?" *Management-Issues*, July 9, 2009, http://www.management-issues.com/2009/7/9/research/the-mba-oath-a-new-era-of-responsibility.asp.

EPILOGUE

1. J. Q. Wilson, "Capitalism and Morality," *Public Interest* 121 (Fall 1995): 42–60.

Index

Sign the Oath

The oath on the following page is for you to sign and keep. To become an official signatory of the MBA Oath, log on to www.mbaoath.org.

If you would like to start a student chapter of the MBA Oath movement at your school, please contact us at info@mbaoath.org.

THE MBA OATH

As a manager, my purpose is to serve the greater good by bringing together people and resources to create value that no single individual can create alone. Therefore I will seek a course that enhances the value my enterprise can create for society over the long-term. I recognize my decisions can have far-reaching consequences that affect the well-being of individuals inside and outside my enterprise, today and in the future. As I reconcile the interests of different constituencies, I will face difficult choices.

Therefore I promise:

I will act with utmost integrity and pursue my work in an ethical manner.

I will safeguard the interests of my shareholders, coworkers, customers, and the society in which we operate.

I will manage my enterprise in good faith, guarding against decisions and behavior that advance my own narrow ambitions but harm the enterprise and the societies it serves.

I will understand and uphold, both in letter and in spirit, the laws and contracts governing my own conduct and that of my enterprise.

I will take responsibility for my actions, and I will represent the performance and risks of my enterprise accurately and honestly.

I will develop both myself and other managers under my supervision so that the profession continues to grow and contribute to the well-being of society.

I will strive to create sustainable economic, social, and environmental prosperity worldwide.

I will be accountable to my peers and they will be accountable to me for living by this oath.

This oath I make freely, and upon my honor.

_____

SIGNATURE

_____

NAME   DATE